"This book is a powerful meditation by a dedicated Catholic. It combines a rich expertise in philosophy, an impressive familiarity with Catholic theology, and a passionate concern for the life of faith in our day. The provocative presentation, combined with helpful discussion questions, makes this a useful stimulus for the reflections of Catholic laity. Dick Westley is an inspiring Catholic layman and scholar."

Rev. Timothy E. O'Connell, Ph.D.
Director, Institute of Pastoral Studies
Loyola University of Chicago

"If you are an American who is often uncomfortable because you tend to 'see' things somewhat differently from the way the institutional aspect of the Roman Catholic church 'sees' them, then this is the book for you. It is a book that...enhances the dignity of being human... helps make sense out of the traditional Christian belief that God's spirit is indeed with the creatures she has created...and sees value in human experiences communally funded. In fact, these experiences are so valuable because they are revelatory—and as such take precedence over law.

"To be an American and to be Catholic at the same time, i.e., faithful to what American values teach and what Catholic values teach, is often apparently contradictory...but it can be done; and this book suggests how.

"The reader may not agree with everything the author says but he or she will certainly be challenged to think over many traditional stances of the Roman Catholic church. The section on 'faithful dissent' is invaluable. This effort to restore the rightful place of the *sensus fidelium* in Catholic teaching is long overdue!

"No matter what the reader thinks about the delicate matters Dick Westley touches upon, he or she will undoubtedly conclude on a note of hope with the author that 'now is *not* the time to leave' (the Roman Catholic church) because, despite appearances, the Roman Catholic church is on the verge of becoming for the first time in its history truly 'catholic.'"

Dr. Aidan A. Licari
Director, Toolen Institute for Parish Services

Dick Westley

A Theology of Presence

The Search for Meaning in the American Catholic Experience

TWENTY-THIRD PUBLICATIONS
Mystic, Connecticut

"A Parable," by Francis Sullivan, is soon to appear in a book of parables written by the same author and published by Harper & Row.

Twenty-Third Publications
185 Willow Street
P.O. Box 180
Mystic CT 06355
(203) 536-2611

ISBN 0-89622-373-6
Library of Congress Catalog Card Number 88-72012

Other Books by Dick Westley

Redemptive Intimacy:
A New Perspective for the Journey to Adult Faith

Morality and Its Beyond

CONTENTS

A Theology of Presence

INTRODUCTION

In his one-man play entitled *I Would Be Called John,* Eugene Kennedy puts these words in the mouth of Angelo Roncalli on the eve of his election as Pope John XXIII:

> Let me tell you, of all the confessions I have listened to, I have not heard sin nearly so much as I have heard discouragement. Discouragement of themselves, and of life. *Discouragement is what truly kills people.* And it is not their failings, especially not those of the flesh, although some priests speak of nothing else, they regard these people as sinners. Jesus himself understood and forgave these readily. No, it is their discouragement with life. Such people want to do good, but they always seem to have nothing but trouble and disappointment and suffering, sickness of all kinds, the death of children, the everyday hurts and disappointments of life. Think of the pain of those people who have nobody to love. And also think of the pain of those who do.

And later in the play, after the election, good Pope John says this:

> The reason I will call this Council, and what the Bishops can help in, is not something abstract, no, not at all. *It is simply to make the human sojourn on earth a little less sad.*

These two statements pretty well capture why I am once again writing, to speak out against the growing discouragement of our people, young and old, with the faith enterprise in the United States. I wish to contribute something positive, if I can, to making the human journey on earth in our days a "little less sad."

The growing discouragement and sadness among believing American Catholics is not without cause or reason. It stems from who we are. That is to say, it arises precisely from the fact that we are "American" *and* "Catholic." Those of us who were born both American and Catholic cannot help but think of ourselves as fortunate and truly blessed by God. We have thought of ourselves, at least until recently, as the envy of the whole world: We are citizens of the greatest nation on the earth, and members of the one *true* church.[1] An unbeatable combination. And so we walked this earth as if we owned it, like a race of giants, heads held high, confident in our demeanor and bearing, making our superiority felt, aware that children of a lesser god would give anything to be in our shoes. No more. Such a conception of ourselves is no longer possible. All is not well either with America, the Catholic church, or with ourselves for that matter.

America's streets are dotted with the homeless ones; native Americans continue to be exploited and oppressed; all of the poor are struggling as never before in this nation of plenty; women are still second-class citizens and constitute the poorest of America's poor; the disabled and aged are warehoused out of sight; unemployment is increasing; the State imprisons Christians active in the peace and sanctuary movements while allowing hardened criminals to openly ply their dark trades; and more of our national budget is invested in nuclear devices and weapons that common sense and decency tell us is unconscionable. And while all this is going on, the majority of Americans seem unconcerned, busily pursuing their individual interests—a sure sign of the isolation and indifference that permeate the America of our day.

After Vatican II, there was a new spirit among Catholics, a spirit that was to have heralded a new age—of open windows, and new possibilities and greater commitment to the dream of the Kingdom. And who can deny that all these things have happened to some degree? But suddenly, the church of Rome has become fearful. There is a new repressive spirit emerging, and the church of North America is suddenly viewed as disobedient, if not downright schismatic, and badly in need of discipline and reform. Bishops, such as Archbishop Hunthausen of Seattle, who reach out pastorally to their people in new ways, are operating under what resembles "house-arrest" in their own dioceses. Our theologians, like Charles Curran, are under attack, and always because they cannot support in conscience the obviously inadequate sexual morality of the institutional church. Women are not only held to be second class Christians, but are blatantly told,"God wants it that way." The young are alienated from and disinterested in the institutional church. And adult Catholics more and more are succumbing to the blandishments of the secular American culture, which translates into the fact that though they remain in the church, they really have no taste, desire, or incentive for the Lord's dream of transforming this world into the Kingdom.

Many of us are sorely divided in our very souls. Those of us who are no longer young, and not quite yet old, are struggling to make sense of our own lives against this backdrop of unrest and upheaval within the two great institutions that have formed and fashioned us since our earliest days. For in the end, we *are* Americans, and we *are* Catholic. How best to put these two, at times contradictory, things together within the confines of a single life and yet remain faithful to the best in each dream is the unmet challenge of our lives.

Like everyone else, I have experienced the great pain and confusion of being an American Catholic these days, but strangely enough I have managed not to succumb to cynicism. When I ask myself why that is, and how it has been possible for me not to lose heart and avoid what so many of my friends are experiencing, the answer that keeps emerging is *because of what I have learned from my own life journey.* It is my thought that because this has been helpful to me in these difficult days, then perhaps I should share it with others in the hope that they, too, might find some relief from the smothering sadness and discouragement that mark our days. In offering the following reflections, this is my earnest hope.

Of course, such an approach to this book makes portions of it obviously autobiographical. To share what one has learned from experience is inevitably to share something of one's own story. There was one very special experience that was the inspiration for the writing of this book. It served to galvanize the otherwise disorganized jumble of thoughts running through my mind into some sort of unified whole. It was one of those peak experiences that occurs unforeseen, unbidden in an instant, and then is over, leaving in its wake a profound realization of truth that affects one ever after. It has left its mark on both the author and this book.

Discovering the Centrality of "Presence"

A while ago, I was asked to address the National Lay Ministry Association at their annual convention in Minneapolis. The gracious invitation was accompanied by a strong caveat against my giving anything like a prepared talk. "We're trying to get away from that sort of thing. Just share your thoughts with us, the thing you're working on at present. We find that works best." When I said that I was a bit uncomfortable with so loose a format for a national convention, the reply was that all I need do then was to make an outline, but definitely no prepared talk.

As the months went by I worked every week on my little outline, trying to pick just the right word or phrase to trigger my failing memory when I was up in front of the convention. The outline underwent many changes until I was reasonably confident that I had given myself sufficient cues to share effectively what I had to say. I worked last on the outline about a week before the convention, and congratulated myself at having gotten everything in order so far in advance. Usually I'm rushing around at the end.

Well, as things turned out, I ended up doing my usual last minute cramming in spite of my best intentions. I came home from school the day before I was to fly to Minneapolis overwhelmed by the realization that I was not at all comfortable with the situation. I was going to have to write the talk out to be comfortable about it. But there was no time. I felt like an undergraduate student who had waited until the last minute to do an important assignment.

There was no time to think, no time to produce a polished document—the agenda was to get something written out, get anything written out, just get it done so you can catch your flight and give the paper. No time, even, to worry about how bad it might be.

The family had long since gone to bed, but I was glued to the computer trying to transform the single words and phrases of my outline into paragraphs. And then it happened. At two or three in the morning as I was typing feverishly, I had suddenly typed a line that caused me to stop cold, and to stare transfixed at the screen. The silence was deep and profound, in sharp contrast to the clattering of the keys that had filled the air just seconds before. It was a sacred kind of silence, the kind of silence one associates with the generation of an insight, with a revelatory moment. Suddenly all the rushing stopped, and time seemed unimportant. In fact, I must have sat there staring for about twenty minutes or so, staring at these words on the screen: *"I have called you to live out your lives in the 'presence' of one another, and I pledge Myself to live out My life in 'your' presence."*

The jubilation of savoring so revelatory a line soon gave way to absolute panic. What it meant was that I would have to scrap everything I had written and start over, centering my talk on the beautiful truth I had inadvertently stumbled upon alone in my room in the small hours of the morning. But I had no choice. I felt called, compelled to flesh it out.

Feverishly working until daylight, I did exactly that. Applying the insight of "presence" to only two of many possible themes: Christian spirituality and human sexuality. What effect does the fact that God has pledged to live out the very life of the Godhead in our presence have on the traditional ways of thinking and talking about each of those themes? These questions constituted the heart of my talk, and those reflections form the core of Chapters One and Two of this book.

My thoughts turned to Soren Kierkegaard who remarked about how insulting it was to attempt to prove the existence of God.[2] To him that was an unthinkable enterprise. He likened it to trying to prove the existence of your spouse or your child when they were standing right in front of you. How silly to attempt to prove the existence of someone *in their very presence.* But that is what the philosophers attempt to do when they try to prove or disprove the existence of God. How convoluted to have someone ignore God's presence in life, thereby becoming unsure of God's existence, and then attempt to overcome that self-induced uncertainty by trying to *prove* that existence, all the while God being *present.* God is present...nothing more need be said about that. What calls out for our attention, reflection, and discussion are the unbelievable consequences of that presence in our everyday lives.

At the convention, the talk went well enough. The excitement I had experienced the day before seemed contagious and the question period that followed the presentation was electric. I didn't have the heart to tell my audience that just hours before I had been where they were now and that I had no real advantage in understanding what I had just said to them.

Further Reflections on "Presence"

After the urgency of preparing a talk for the convention, things settled down to a less frenetic and less urgent pace. But my "one-liner" remained vivid and energizing as I found time to think about its further implications. It occurred to me that one might be able to re-cast much of Catholic theology in terms of the fact that God has pledged "to live out My life in *your* presence." Far too many of us continue to feel that we have to struggle amid and against all the distractions of life to find the time and the opportunity to get in touch with God, as if just living hampers or lessens our God relationship. Much of what passes for "spirituality" is undoubtedly based on such false assumptions. It is true that the Christian tradition warns against the "seduction of the world." In that it is undoubtedly correct, but is there something we are missing? What if it is not so much the pleasures and allurements of the world that it warns us against, but not really living? For we read in the Talmud: "In the world to come, each of us will be called to account for all the good things God put on earth which we refused to enjoy." What would we say about spiritual life were we to recast our thoughts about it in terms of God's pledged presence *in our very lives*? I try to make a beginning on this in Chapter One.

If we have misunderstood our spiritual life, then it would be truly surprising if we were able to speak the truth about our bodies and our sex life. What would human sexuality look like if it too were recast in terms of the theology of presence? What is the role of the body in the work of love? The work of the Kingdom? That is the central issue in Chapter Two.

If one dares to go against what is called "traditional" teaching in matters of the spiritual life and sex, on what grounds can this be attempted? Only because God's presence in our everyday experiences gives us a source of revelation to which even Scriptural and magisterial authority must face up. The theology of presence casts new light on the revelatory power of experience and the subsequent recasting of our notions of authority. A discussion on this is to be found in Chapter Three.

The theology of presence has some salutary effects when applied to our notion of salvation. Supposedly people are in the church precisely to better guarantee "salvation"—whatever that means. And in the post-Vatican II church there is much ambiguity about what it does mean. This is due to the fact that, of the many possible theological accounts of salvation available in our scriptural and theological tradition, we seem to have adopted the most rigid, the most juridical, the most frightening of all the possibilities. What the theology of presence can do is to open our minds to those other accounts, and to convince us that in the end whatever account we give must be compatible with our experience of God's presence among us, a presence meant to reconcile the whole world to its Maker (Chapter Four).

Community is, quite paradoxically, both the result and the pre-requisite of salvation. This is because community is the incarnation of that reconciliation which *is* salvation. The reason for so much talk about community these days is that we have finally come to understand that community *is* "the saving place." Our attempts at community are a novitiate and preparation for salvation/reconciliation both here and hereafter (Chapter Five).

The three final chapters are concerned with the conflict we are all experiencing in trying to be both American *and* Catholic. It is generally assumed that there is a deep-seated conflict between the American Dream and the Kingdom for which we all work and pray. This assumption is not without evidence, and Chapter Six is an account of the prevailing value of our culture that seems inevitably opposed to the Kingdom: individualism. The American experience is revelatory of a deep malaise for which the theology of presence seems particularly suited.

After having spoken so long, and perhaps so abstractly, about the importance of "presence," Chapter Seven presents a parable by Francis P. Sullivan, S.J., which presents the theology of presence in very illuminating and concrete terms. But the parable does much more than that. It also shows the direction of an answer to such questions as: Is it possible to be both American *and* Catholic? Why be Catholic? What does it really mean to be Catholic? The issues clustered around these questions are what constitute the core of Chapter Eight.

Finally, mindful of the need for dialogue and sharing of important faith issues, and because people have found this feature helpful in my earlier books, I have supplied dialogue questions for the sections of each chapter.

CHAPTER ONE

A THEOLOGY OF PRESENCE

I have been in ministry religious education all of my adult life, and for the past years have been struggling to find the words to articulate what I have come to see as the central truth of Christian faith, *i.e..*, incarnation. Trying to communicate this unbelievable truth, and to identify some of its more important consequences is what I attempted in my two most recent books: *Redemptive Intimacy* and *Morality and Its Beyond.* Still, I never could get it said tersely enough for my satisfaction. Then, as I recounted in the Introduction, the insight I had been struggling for a decade and a half to find, slipped out unnoticed while I was typing and thinking of something else. It has come to be for me the heart and essence of Christianity: *"I have called you to live out your lives in the 'presence' of one another, and I pledge Myself to live out My life in your presence."*

Since this sums up all the theology I know, this little book too has no other message. Indeed, at those moments when I am feeling particularly energized by this statement, I become somewhat dogmatic and am tempted to assert that not only is it all the theology *I* know, *it is all the theology there is, period.*

Of course, the truth of my one-liner is not new, indeed it is very old, going all the way back to ancient Israel. In fact, it is Israel's most important bequest to the human race. That is why Christian anti-Semitism is something of a mystery to me. In the light of Israel's tremendous contribution to the human race, one would think that Jews would be revered and honored for what their tradition has kept alive particularly for Christians.

As Christians, we tell the story that somehow God was revealed in a special way to Israel. Not true. From the start, God was self-revealing to *all* of humankind. This is God's nature. This is what it means to be Spirit. *It was ancient Israel that first caught on,* that first came to the realization that God does not dwell in some far-off place, but with humankind. So it was that Israel was the laughing stock of the ancient world because, then as now, "everyone knows" God/gods dwell in inaccessible splendor beyond the pale of this world. And then as now, those who say otherwise are looked upon as strange and fanatical. We owe ancient Israel much. Pius XII spoke great wisdom to Christians when he said that "spiritually we are *all* Semites."

Christians/Catholics have long since forgotten their Jewish roots. Indeed, most of Christian morality and spirituality seem to be inspired more by the vision of God and human life going back to the venerable Greek philosopher, Plato, than by the God whom Israel came to recognize as "present."

The Mystery of Presence

Presence is a mystery. We use all sorts of words to try to capture it, words like "charisma," "charm," "magnetism," "ambience," "attraction." Philosophers, like Gabriel Marcel, struggle hard to unpack the meaning of such words only to find in the end that they cannot be captured solely in words, but can only be pointed to in experience. The Old Testament, too, encounters the mystery of "presence," especially in its relations with Yahweh. And it, too, attempts to capture it in words *and* stories, telling of Yahweh's faithfulness and commitment to Israel in the Covenant. Even though the words are inadequate, we all soon come to *know* what "presence" is, because it is one of life's earliest lessons.

In the words of Marcel, presence "refreshes my inner being, reveals me to myself, makes me more fully myself than I should be if I were not exposed to its impact."[3] That is what it means to be spirit—to be capable of discerning the presence of another spirit, as well as of being presence for another. Presence is both the nature and the work or vocation of spirit, and as such is the essence or heart of what we call "the spiritual life" or "spirituality." Far from calling us to flee from or abandon the world, our faith calls us to be really and truly "present" to it.

Thanks to ancient Israel, we know what that means. The Israelites' account of Yahweh's covenanted presence to them as a people is the definitive model of what it means to be spirit, and what spirituality is really all about. Presence envelops the other in caring concern, it is not only "being there," it is not even only "being there with," it is both of these and most importantly "being there for." Presence creates a freeing space, a nurturing ambiance, a solidarity, a communion, a connectedness without which spirits shrivel, become impotent, and eventually stagnate. I need not list all the dimensions of Yahweh's presence to ancient Israel, for they are well known to all of us. Suffice it to say that owing to that continued "presence" the work of spirit continues to go on among us today.

What It Means to Be "Incarnate Spirit"

In order to understand how the work of spirit goes on among the likes of us human beings, we shall have to spend some time reflecting on the human condition, entering into, as briefly and painlessly as I can manage it, the obfuscating world of metaphysics. But bear with me, because the insight is crucial and fascinating, and it changes everything. The insight did not originate with me, but with Thomas Aquinas. Yet the insight's provenance does not make it a traditional view. The truth is that Aquinas's genius has been ignored on this issue.

For Aquinas, human beings are not animals, not even "rational" ones. Though he accepted the Aristotelian definition of the human person, he did not think that "animal" was our proper genus. If one wants to classify humans one has no alternative but to eschew the genus "animal" for the more appropriate genus "spirit." The specifying difference distinguishing human beings from "pure" spirits is that we are "incarnate," that is to say "enfleshed" spirits. To place human beings in the genus "animal" is to commit a category mistake. It is to be fooled by appearances, by the fact that, like the higher animals, we have a genotype, visceral organs, genitals, and a digestive tract. But the significance of this similarity is misplaced and lost, unless one has some notion of the overall economy of the human person, an economy which Aquinas consistently taught was *totally spiritual.*

According to the Platonic account, which became the Christian account since all of the Church Fathers were Platonists, matter lies completely outside the domain of spirit. Even when they are joined, it is only by accident because of a fall of some sort on the part of spirit. And so the war between matter and spirit goes on. The human soul/spirit is hampered and at risk while in matter, and so death is the liberation of the human spirit from the prison of the body. Aquinas sees it otherwise.

For Aquinas, human beings are all and totally spirit, but are lowest in the order of spirits. That is to say, human beings are so low in the order of spirits that *in order to perfect themselves as spirit, they must be immersed in matter. Far from being a hindrance to spirit, matter is humankind's means of reaching spiritual perfection.* Soul and body are joined in so intimate a union within the human person, that Aquinas says not only does the human soul make the body live, it makes the body live by the soul's own spiritual life. Despite all appearances to the contrary there is none other than a spiritual life in human beings. And in that one life, the role of the human body is precisely to enable the human spirit to do the work of spirit, which we have seen is "presence."

Aquinas really means what he says. So true is it that matter/body is essential to the spiritual perfection of an "incarnate spirit," that death is not in itself a liberation of the human spirit, but is its total impoverishment. Without body, the human spirit cannot operate as spirit at all, cannot do the work of spirit, and so Aquinas felt that God would by Divine Influx make up to the impoverished human spirit for the lack of its body—at least until they were once again rejoined at the end.

Aquinas's position is so radical and revolutionary that to this day it has not gained anything resembling widespread acceptance. Yet if his perspective is legitimate, and I believe it is, it changes everything.

Aquinas identifies the "work of spirit" as knowing/understanding and loving. On the basis of his hypothesis, it follows that human beings can do neither without body. All attempts by humankind at a purely spiritual knowing or loving are not only wrong-headed, but futile. If we aspire to know and love each other, if we aspire to really be present to one another, then we must understand that as "incarnate" spirits we can only do this physically, incarnately, enfleshedly. More than that, if we aspire to know and love God, even then we can only do so incarnately, through our bodies. That is the price we pay for being lowest in the order of spirits. But fear not, the human body was created and fashioned as it is, precisely to enable and empower us to be fully human and to do the work of reconciliation, the very work of spirit. The human body, as anyone who has worked in healthcare knows, is marvelously suited to its "spiritual" tasks. It is not only a "biological" wonder, it is a "spiritual" marvel as well.

Consider the human face. In the human face more than anywhere else we encounter the mystery of our humanness: *presence*. It is there that we encounter the wonder of spirit-enfleshed. It is in the countenances of one another; in the eyes, the smile, the look, the glance, that we either see the invitation to live out our relatedness and bondedness to one another, or the fearful rejection of that dream. And the human voice, which issues from that face, is itself an instrument of spirit. A word, a phrase, a tone all communicate in hidden ways what lies beneath the surface in the very heart and soul and spirit of a human being. And what of the human hand as an instrument of spirit? The warm firm grasp of hands in friendship, the caressing hands of lovers, the caring hands of those who minister to human needs, the helpful hands of neighbors, the prayerful hands of worship...all convey a reality which goes far beyond the physical.

But there is a deadly trade-off built into the bargain. Aquinas asked why it was that an immortal soul should be joined to an organic body. Wouldn't it be better if an incarnate spirit were joined to matter which more closely resembled the soul in its indestructibility? Why not an inorganic body of granite, of diamonds? His answer is that in order to give the lowest sort of spirit access to knowledge and love, a body that is equipped with sense organs, and even sex organs is needed. The consequence of this, of course, is that it is fragile and has only the most precarious of holds on existence. So the paradox of a spirit having to face death is itself the direct result of the spirit's need to be "incarnate" in order to do the work of spirit.

Given what has been said, *we have only two things at our disposal with which to do the work of the spirit,* to do the work of presence, to do the work of relatedness, love and solidarity, to do the work of the Kingdom. And when Jesus was among us, though God he be for Christians, he too, as human, as an incarnate spirit, had only those same two things with which to accomplish his mission of reconciliation among us. And what are these two things? Our *words* and *physical presence,* of course.

It is because we know so much about Jesus that we perhaps understand too little. It is as if the transfiguration and resurrection have made us ignorant of the real import of Jesus' human presence among us. Perhaps we have to put aside all that former ages have said about the divinity of Jesus and put ourselves in the shoes of his first disciples. They had to struggle with ambiguity, uncertainty, unknowing, and had only their experience of Jesus in his humanness to go on. And of course, on Jesus' side the only means he had to accomplish his mission were his human, corporeal presence, and his spoken words. And to this day these are the only things we humans have, both for mediating the superabundance of God's unconditional love for humankind to one another, and for having what traditionally has been called a "spirituality." We make an abiding mistake, and sorely deceive ourselves whenever we think otherwise.

Conclusion

If there is a conclusion to be drawn from what I have said, I would suggest that it is this. A rigid spiritualism has plagued the Christian faith throughout its history. It seems that someone is always trying to over-spiritualize the faith enterprise out of fear. Fear of life, fear of love, fear of bonding, fear of emotions, fear of body, fear of sex. That fear causes them, following the lead of Plato and the ancient Stoics, to set up two worlds: one of body and matter, and the other of soul and spirit. But there is only one God. And there is only one world. In fact there is only one reality—*Spirit in the World*—to use Karl Rahner's happy phrase. So we should stop talking about the "spiritual" life. We should talk rather about "life" and of our God who is incarnate there, revealing to us in our experience all we need to know in order to, like God, *be truly present* to one another and to our world. For if there is such a thing as Christian spirituality, it is the spirituality of presence, and it is readily available to everyone regardless of state or station. But we must never forget that we can only "be present" to God and to one another through our bodies. This is what it means to be human, to be an incarnate spirit.

CHAPTER TWO

SEX AND THE CONTEMPORARY FAMILY

The benefits of "family" seem so obvious, so precious, so important to human life that it is quite understandable that we have come to romanticize family life. And once having done this, we then assess the present state of family life in this country and wonder why it has fallen on such hard times. Many think that the American family is being destroyed by economics. Getting a job, doing what it takes to "get ahead," have exacted a terrible toll on family life—and one does not have to look very far to see this. But I am convinced that, despite the negative impact on family life of American economic values, family life has always been a very precarious enterprise. It is just that in our day we have come to know more about how families *really* work. In the light of that new knowledge and understanding we could justify putting a warning label on every marriage certificate—just as we do on cigarettes. *Warning: Families Can Be Dangerous to Your Health,* especially your psychological health. The fact is, families have *always* been a "mixed" blessing. It is just that contemporary American life seems to have exacerbated the negatives to such a degree that many young adults now say they really don't want children.

The Family Crucible

Dan Berrigan once characterized the nuclear age as: "...an age of the disintegration of common understanding. It has to do with the nuke as a symbol of the break-up of human relationships: spouse from spouse, friend from friend, lover from lover. It has to do with the breakup of a common consciousness about what is precious to all of us...."[4]

It is in this sense that one can speak of the "nuclear" family long before the advent of nuclear weapons. At the heart of every human family is the basic clash of wills, the conflict of differing value systems, the struggle between dependence and autonomy, and most significantly the challenge of relating sexually. Viewed in this way, the tone of the nuclear age is just the final and ultimate expression of what has been at the heart of human families from the beginning, *conflict.* In our day it is all coming out in an increase of divorce, wife and child beatings, incest, and the sexual abuse of minor children. In our age, more than ever before, families are being torn apart because their members foster the natural conflict-mechanisms within the family while at the same time resisting or abusing its natural bonding mechanisms.

Consider the situation of young adults within the family group. Typically, by the time they reach 25-30 years of age, their parents have come to the mid-life passage. Everything in the family is very volatile. The young person is seeking her/his independence, and the parents are having trouble coping with their struggles to find their own identity in a relationship of many years. As Napier and Whitaker put it, by mid-life

"The marriage begins to feel like a trap. So the couple begins to back away from each other, mistrusting. They are right to mistrust. How can you safely depend on someone with whom you're struggling for dominance in the relationship?"[5]

If there is any truth to this statement, we must surmise that the family situation that nurtured children no longer exists by the time these children become young adults. And it no longer exists because they are no longer dependent and have moved into their own adulthood, and because things are not quite the way they were between their parents, who are struggling to redefine their own roles and identity in a family that may well seem to have swallowed them up. So at the very time when they are thirsting for independence and striving to find their own way, their parents are reassessing their own lives and trying to find a new identity without destroying the family unit.

When parents and young adults are simultaneously going through a time of real crisis in their lives, it is very difficult for them to nurture and effectively tend to their intergenerational relationships. Yet, that is the way family life is: people clustered on a journey which takes them in divergent directions, but which keeps them bonded to one another in the most intimate and precarious of relationships. And each family member is asked to discern in his or her own life just how much independence and how much gift of self to the family group is possible. Yes, we tend to romanticize families because of the good things that come from them, but we also know first hand that being a family member remains the most challenging of our roles, both as parent and as offspring.

Sensitive to the difficulties of family life, the institutional church has championed the importance and sacredness of familial relations. But however ardently it preaches of family values, and however conscientiously and with the best of intentions it attempts to promote them, the fact is that the Catholic church is unconsciously and inadvertently one of the most anti-family institutions on the face of the earth. And it will remain so, until it gives up its Platonic ways, realizes the significance of "human" sexual relations between spouses for the good of the family, and finds the graciousness to proclaim the true meaning of human sexuality.

The Meaning of "Human" Sexuality

Sexually active believers are caught between two diametrically opposed views, *neither of which is validated by their experience.* On the one side is the secular culture which reduces sexual activity to an athletic event or recreation. On the other side is the Catholic church which continues to put forth moral norms of Platonic origin and to teach that procreation is so integral to human sexuality that any sexual activity not open to it must be judged morally wrong.

1. American Culture's Story on Sex and Sexuality Several sectors of our culture would have us believe that sex is simply a matter of fun and games. They suggest that the primary and perhaps the only meaning that human sexual activity can have is pleasure. Sex is to be used "recreationally"—just as liquor and drugs are. The male animal, in particular, has always tried to convince himself and anyone else who would listen that this is just the way it is.

For example, in 1970 Professor Robert Tyler wrote: "Let us agree that *marriage is impossible.* It has *always* been an impossible institution. In all its many forms, it has clamped some kind of social control on sex to make fun and games serve such stuffy values as child-rearing, the inheritance of wealth, or the transmission of social status and tradition. But sex has always burst the boundaries! *American marriage has been especially impossible.* From the beginning Americans frowned on all those extra-marital sports discovered by older and wiser cultures to make the institution livable. The strain in American marriage, of course, has been terrific. In the early phases of our present sexual revolution after World War I, the cracks in the old, crumbling edifice were papered over by well-meaning romantics who wrote marriage manuals. By now attempts to save the institution have become pretty desperate. Already one can see the future taking shape in the experiments of the present college-age generation, which has apparently decided to deal with the institution by ignoring it as an anachronism and hypocrisy."[6] And in 1985, some 15 years later, Robert Bellah proclaimed: "The present ideology of 'individualism' has difficulty justifying why men and women should be giving themselves to one another at all."[7]

In the past, there were dissenting voices to this rather male-chauvinist view of marriage from some women. Our culture has been so persuasive in its campaign to get all to view sex as "fun and games" that now, as often as not, it is women who voice the culture's cry in this regard. Marriage is looked down on—because it attempts to put a more significant and human meaning to sexual activity. The air is filled with pornography—it abounds in books, movies, song lyrics—and we are constantly bombarded with sexual stimuli and invited to "get with it." Those who raise their voices in dissent are ridiculed as being "old fashioned." The modern American sexual dictum is that people have a right to do as they please sexually, and it is nobody's business but their own. This is the story American culture constantly puts forth and attempts to "sell" to us. This cultural attitude is patently absurd, blatantly dehumanizing, and offensive.

2. *The Catholic Story About Sex and Sexuality* Across this planet, people who know little else about the Catholic church know at least this one thing: the Catholic church vigorously proclaims and authoritatively teaches that sex is for making babies. So committed to this position is the church of Rome, that it goes on to say that to engage in sexual activity which willfully and voluntarily intervenes in the possibility of making a baby, is a violation of sex's intrinsic meaning and hence is always immoral.

How did sex and procreation come to be inextricably linked in the Catholic mind? In the second century, certain Christians called Gnostics were so impressed with the Lord's apparent endorsement of celibacy that they began teaching that sexual intercourse, and even marriage, were forbidden to those who wanted to walk with the Lord. The traditional view on sex as we now know it arose from a defense the church mounted against this extreme position of the Gnostics. Without doubt Scripture endorsed celibacy, but it also endorsed marriage, saying that it was good. But Scripture did not give any reason why sex and marriage were good. So the teaching church began to look for an answer to that "why" question.

They found it in the philosophical teachings of the Stoics. A thing is good only to the degree that it fulfills its purpose. So obviously sex was not evil in itself if it could be found to have a good purpose. Offspring were obviously the good purpose that justified followers of Jesus not being celibate. Helpful in arguing against the extreme position of the Gnostics, this way of arguing also gave the impression, an impression finally explicitly stated by St. Augustine, that sex could only be good if it were both open to procreation and engaged in with procreative intent. How ironic, then, that the institutional church, in trying to defend and protect the "goodness" of sexual activity, actually gave rise to a line of reasoning that has, from the earliest days, put sexual activity under a cloud of suspicion, and led the church into a posture that is not only counter-intuitive, but wrong. And to realize this fact, one need only think of how out of character it would be for Jesus to talk about sex the way the Catholic church has for almost two millennia, as John Paul II has unceasingly from the first days of his pontificate. And it does not help to call such a teaching "traditional," meaning it has been taught for a long time, because it has been wrong for exactly the same amount of time.

Still, we can ask why the teaching church is so insistent on this matter, and why it can't simply admit it has been wrong-headed in tying human sexual activity totally and exclusively to procreation. I fear that the reason is that this teaching on human sexuality does not stand alone; it is the logical result of a certain mindset about the condition of humankind, the meaning of human life, the significance of Christian faith, and the role and nature of ecclesial authority. In short, the church can hardly give up its teaching on human sexuality without giving up its whole understanding of what Christianity is all about. That is why we find the teaching church so adamant and unbending on sexual issues. It understands that much more is at stake than sex. But no matter how vigorously the institutional church tries to urge the traditional position, every day it is being directly contradicted in the conjugal experiences of its members. In such circumstances it becomes *very* difficult, if not impossible, to tell a believable story about sex. In addition, there is silence on sexual issues by lay people, because Catholics have never been allowed to trust their own experience as a source of truth and light. Like children, we seem to wait to be told, told by "those who really know." But the fact is, that those who claim really to know, don't.

The truth of the matter is that the Catholic tradition on sex has very little to do with faith, and is almost an unchanged expression of what the pagan Stoics of ancient Rome believed. And so it is that we have been for too long saddled with an inadequate and erroneous sexual morality. It is time for sexually active believers to proclaim in God's name, and without fear, what they have learned in bed—confident that it is, when communally funded, as authoritative as any episcopal letter. No matter how vigorously the institutional church tries to urge the traditional position, that position continues to be directly contradicted every day in the lived experiences of its members. Consequently, a deep division has developed between the teaching church and its believing members on this issue. What does experience reveal about the meaning of human sexuality?

3. "Having Sex" vs. "Making Love" Let me present a few of the many things which have convinced me that human sex is primarily *relational,* having little or nothing to do with biological procreation, having everything to do with human bonding. First of all, if human sex were primarily procreational, then we would expect that humans would become sexually aroused only at times of fertility, much as happens among other animals. But, as has been suggested, the human person is fully and totally *spirit,* albeit an impoverished one. So to limit human sexuality to its biological function is to overlook the fact that in humans the most significant sex power is spiritual—the human mind. We can become sexually aroused at will. That can be troublesome, of course. But the fact is that if, as we have seen, the primary work of body is knowing and loving presence, then sexual arousal must be viewed in relation to these primary ends of an inspirited body.

This may strike you as an esoteric conclusion, drawn from the even more esoteric metaphysical principles discussed earlier. Perhaps. But we find this same conclusion in the everyday experiences of people, as well as in our everyday language. Language doesn't arise for no reason. What were the original framers of language trying to tell us when they coined the happy phrase "to make love" when speaking of human sexual intercourse? You see, the truth has been there from the start. And experience corroborates it. Anyone can "have sex," but for human sexual intercourse to be "love-making" it must be the work of the spirit. But, as we have seen, this is precisely what it is, this is precisely what God means it to be.

Consider the excessive amount of psychic energy it takes for sex to remain casual. How careful one must be once sexually active. For it is the nature of human sex to make love, to bond you to your lover. "Pleasure seekers" who are into promiscuity must hit and run, for should they tarry the least bit, they could well be caught up in the both painful and rewarding mystery of human sexuality: the spiritual bonding of persons. This is something no libertine wants anything to do with, something an alienated person might be afraid of.

The fact is that sexual activity, when it is truly "love-making" and the work of spirit, is the antithesis of self-indulgence. It is the height of asceticism. Those who have looked at sexually active people as self-indulgent and not pure and undefiled enough to be spiritual have perpetrated a horrendous lie. While it may be true that "pleasure seekers" use sex for their own interests, *this is not the nature of human sexuality*. This is a rejection of truly human sexuality, which is always spiritual, in favor of a lesser reality.

These are some of the things which experience teaches us about human sexuality, and those who are sexually active in "love-making" ways have no difficulty recognizing it as an authentic spirituality. For in the end, what is spirituality? It is nothing less than the life of spirit, open and gracious, giving and caring, loving and sharing. As "incarnate" spirits, we can only do all this through the mediation of our bodies. Human sexuality at its best, *is* spirituality. This truth has been known to Christians for centuries; they have learned it from their own sexual experiences, but have remained silent about it. They have remained silent because were they to have spoken, they would have suffered recriminations and rejection from the church.

Beset as we are by a culture gone sexually mad, we can not remain silent any longer. The young depend on those of us who are sexually active to say some words of wisdom to them about what it means to be human, and sexually active. We cannot turn away in embarrassment. We must begin to share with them what we have learned about love-making from our own sexual experiences in order to discover what is communally funded about them. If we remain silent, our young people will have to turn to other models.

What It Means to "Make Love"

Given the pornographic and licentious tone of contemporary life, some will see my claim about human sexuality as just one more reason for self-indulgence. Given the current revival of puritanical and fundamentalist religious attitudes in opposition to such licentiousness, others will see my claim as sacrilegious and not "spiritual" enough. In such a climate of misunderstanding, perhaps it is necessary to say just a bit more, but in this as in so many other of life's basic issues experience is the best teacher. Those who are sexually active in love-making ways will know what I am talking about, but find my words inadequate. To those who are sexually active but have never "made love" my words will seem like a foreign language.

Undoubtedly, the simplest and most powerful account of how human love, when it is authentically love, is God-filled, can be found in that marvelous fourth chapter of John's first epistle. "A person without love has known nothing of God, for God *is* love." (4:8) "No one has ever seen God. Yet if we love one another God dwells in us, and God's love is brought to perfection in us." (4:12) "God *is* love, and the one who abides in love, abides in God, and God in him." (4:16)

John is obviously talking very concretely in this epistle, and he never envisioned that Christians of later ages would interpret his words in a Platonic sense, that is, that the love that God is can only be an infinite, disembodied, totally spiritual love. How could he mean this? He says just the opposite. So the concreteness of the love that God *is* and its identification with human love go all the way back to the earliest days of our faith.

It is one thing, however, to affirm that God is love, and quite another to affirm that sexual intercourse, when it is truly human, "makes love" and hence in some sense plugs into God and into the love that God is. This is offensive to "pious ears." God is so perfect, so dispassionate, so beyond the physical, that it seems sacrilegious to suggest that something as earthy, as passionate, as irrational and biological as sexual activity could incarnate God's loving presence. Yet this is precisely what the sexual experience of two millennia of Christianity reveals. How does this work?

It is a profound mystery, so even those who have experienced it can't quite put it into words. But we know when our sexual activity "makes love" and when it doesn't. And there is something very special about those times when it does, so special that once one has experienced it, the penny drops and one finally understands what human sexual relations are really all about. They are about the work of spirit, the work of presence, the work of understanding, the work of love. One feels in solidarity with the beneficent presence which transcends and yet dwells in our world. One feels gifted and graced. One, for however briefly, feels no need to dominate, no need to assert oneself, no need to manipulate, so delicious is the taste of being and of being loved. One feels forgiving and forgiven, at one with God and all of humankind, face to face with not only what is truly good, but with the Goodness which is the hidden source of every other good. One feels oneself to be in a truly saving place and thinks to oneself: "This surely must be what salvation is all about !" With Mother Julian of Norwich, one becomes convinced that: "All shall be well, all shall be well, and all manner of thing shall be well."

Sexual love-making is one of the most difficult of the spiritual arts. Though natural to us, it doesn't seem to come naturally at all. We must learn to do it. Like all the other things of the spirit, it takes practice. But when it happens, it is always a very powerful spiritual experience with profound aftereffects. I am energized, I feel better able to love, I find myself more generous, more giving, more open and less self-conscious. It is of just such stuff that great families are made. Unfortunately, not all families are great. Owing in part, I am sure, to the fact that too many parents, led astray by cultural values, or burdened by erroneous religious ones, most often settle for just "having sex" and only rarely, if ever, "make love." If God wept over the fate of the people of Jerusalem, he must also be in tears over the fate of the growing number of American families built on the shifting sands of "having sex" and not on the firm foundation of human love-making. No wonder the American family is in trouble!

The American Family in Crisis

It has become a commonplace to say that the American family is disintegrating because it has been deprived of the traditional cultural and societal supports of former times, and this precisely at a time when it is beset from without by situations and conditions that erode and disintegrate relational life. I have no desire either to underestimate the truth of this assessment or to rehearse here the long litany of disintegrating forces at work today in our culture. They are well known to all of us. I want simply to reflect on the nature of the family in terms of its sexual center, confident that, if things are right at the center, a family will better resist disintegration both from within and without.

When we think about "families," we Christians again tend to get very Platonic in our thinking. We correctly speak of "love" as the cement of the family, but we don't make the next move, which is to say that the love which cements the family is ultimately an "incarnate" and "enfleshed" love, *i.e.*, a love that human beings "make" sexually. Families depend for their health and wholeness on the sexual activity of the spouses. In the words of America's premier family therapist, Virginia Satir, "The marital relationship is the axis around which all other family relationships are formed. A pained marital relationship tends to produce dysfunctional parenting."[8] To which we might add, "...and dysfunctional parenting more often than not produces dysfunctional family members."

This means that however beset from without by disintegrating forces a family may be, the most disintegrating force of all stems from within the family unit itself, from the pained and unfulfilled sexual relations of the spouses. And as a corollary to that, it follows that the most dangerous external forces for a family are those that undermine the sexual relation that is its center. In that regard, I have already identified two such dangers: the absolutely insane American cultural view of human sexuality; and the absolutely unrealistic and erroneous over-spiritualized view of the magisterial Catholic church. Although other forces erode the family at its edges, these two strike at its very heart. Families will remain at risk from within until the love-making and bonding powers of human sex are fully recognized, prized, and practiced.

The truth and concrete reality of all this is vividly portrayed in a fascinating book by Augustus Napier and Carl Whitaker, *The Family Crucible* (Bantam Books, 1980). The authors tell the story of the Brice family, and take them through two or three years of family therapy. At the beginning, one would swear that "the problem" was the teenage daughter who seems to be completely out of control. I remember the first time I read it, I had harsh feelings toward the daughter, Claudia, and thought I knew that "she" was the real problem. By the time the book ended, it was clear that the real problem was the marital relations of Carolyn and David. The authors, while heavily Freudian, masterfully show how they finally discovered what the "real problem" was, and why and how it was that Claudia's behavior was really a reaction to the pained marital relations of her parents.[9]

The case history shared by Napier and Whitaker is not unique. It is simply a concrete instance of the accepted wisdom uncovered by two decades of study and research by family therapists around the world. And that wisdom comes down to this. Counselling records seem to indicate that problem teenagers are most often (perhaps 70 percent of the time) indications of a troubled marital relationship. That is an amazing statistic, and it corroborates from experience the claim stated earlier that fragmented families are more often than not the by-product of fragmented relations at that family's center.

As the clinical evidence piles up, the Catholic church seems to proceed almost oblivious to the realities of family life. In the name of tradition, it simply refuses to learn from experience. The issue then comes down to this: Must Catholics maintain allegiance to a sexual morality that their everyday experience discredits simply because religious authority proposes it as traditional? Put otherwise: At what point, if ever, in the life of a Catholic Christian is his or her lived experience of life, and of God incarnate in that life, sufficient warrant for dissenting to what ecclesial authority presents as normative? Are Catholics ever to be allowed to grow up? And if there is a time when adult Catholics may, with fear and trembling, make such a move, what would constitute faithful dissent? It is to those issues that we turn next.

CHAPTER THREE

EXPERIENCE AS AUTHORITY

In 1870, the First Vatican Council declared the infallibility of the pope in matters of faith and morals. Ever since, Catholics have generally been divided into two main groups: those who try to extend the scope of that infallibility to the farmost limits, and those who seek legitimate ways and means of interpreting that infallibility in the narrowest sense possible. At the heart of the dispute is a difference of view about the nature of ecclesial authority, and how God acts in, and is present to, the world. It has become a burning question for American Catholics in our times as the church of Rome seems to be on a collision course with the church in the United States. It has reached the point where practically every disagreement is seen as disobedience and a breach in discipline. Talk of schism has even surfaced.

The history of the last 120 years since the declaration of papal infallibility has been marked by the non-malicious, but nonetheless obscene, usurpation and centralization of power (which is not at all the same thing as authority) vested in the pope and the Curia. Concomitant with this, and as a natural by-product, we have witnessed the devaluation of what the tradition calls the *sensus fidelium,* the consensus of all believers, as a vital force in the life of the church.[10]

Lived Experience as Revelatory

Linked to any discussion of authority in the church is the equally important discussion of the role of experience in Christian life. It is wisely said that "experience is the best teacher." But in order to take advantage of the "education" experience offers us at each step of our life journey, we have to be reflective, *i.e.,* give heed to our lives, and be fortunate enough to live long enough. If one, for fear of consequence, always accepts uncritically what culture, the church, the pope, or the Bible say, or if one dies prematurely before experience has finished its lessons, then of course one will have learned little from experience. On the other hand, should one manage to do both—be reflective and live long enough—one will most certainly come to be counted among the wise, and the young will rightly look to that person for such wisdom.

One sure sign of this sort of "wisdom" is the ability of the truly wise among us to tell the communally funded stories (myths) that ground and fashion our common life in ways that are more hope-filled and life-giving than the traditional ways. In this critical and anxious time both for our world and for our church, beset as we are by terror and the rumors of war and the rumors of schism, it is imperative that we avail ourselves of whatever wisdom there may be at our disposal—particularly that which is available within the community on the themes of experience and authority.

Without doubt *life itself* is our best teacher. And I think that mindful Christians not only know this but know *why* it is true. We know from our ancient Jewish roots that our God is the God of life, not death; that God has chosen to live in us, in our deepest parts; and that the divine presence at our very center makes of *our lives* revelation, *i.e.*, sacred shrines from which we may, if only we avail ourselves of the opportunity, learn life's deepest truths. So true is this that we have now come to understand the Bible as itself divine revelation precisely because it arose from the ancient Hebrews' and early Christians' encounter with the Living God in their lives. Whenever we lose sight of this fact, we cannot help but rob life of its revelatory dimension, placing our primary trust elsewhere, *i.e.* in sacred books like the Bible, or in sacred people like the pope.

As we mature and grow older, this lived experience-based truth becomes paramount in our lives. No longer children, we have come to the point where we know that falsehood is falsehood *no matter who generates it*—because we have had access to a source of truth within ourselves distinct from what our religious leaders may say. And if what they say doesn't jibe with the communally-funded experiences of "adult" Christians, the *sensus fidelium*, what they say simply lacks authority. *In the end, it is God-filled human experiences of believing people that are authoritative.*

I had come to that same conclusion back in January 1970, when I wrote a little piece entitled *Experience as Revelatory*, in which I raised the issue as clearly as I could at the time. I find its basic assertions are still valid.

A 1970 Account of the Matter

Traditional Catholicism is authoritarian and so concerned with orthodoxy that it has little or no use for "human experience." In my own experience, educated as I was, I received no indication that Christianity had anything whatsoever to do with experience. The revealed Scriptures, the infallibility of the popes, and the absolute orthodoxy of one's teachers made personal experience practically superfluous. Being a Catholic in the old sense meant complete assurance of the truth or orthodoxy of doctrines and practices simply on the say so of divine or ecclesiastical authority, *without recourse to experience.*

One reason traditional Catholicism ignores experience is its rather limited view of "revelation." Revelation according to traditional teaching ended with the death of the last of the apostles, and not even our infallible popes can add to it substantially. All who come after the apostles can only draw out what was originally revealed. This means that traditional Catholics are a people living in the past, and when their present experiences contradict what teachers taught had been revealed, they feel obliged to ignore their experiences.

Personally, I find it difficult to base my faith on the experience of someone else, no matter what his or her credentials. Doing this tends to produce a faith that is all too easily challenged by new experiences. Yet, this is precisely what many have mistakenly thought we were being asked to do as Catholics. Catholics have tended to look to the Old Testament, to the New Testament, to the theological authorities of the past, and to a long list of infallible popes for the meaning of our faith, and have overlooked the obvious importance of present experience. This has always been a great mistake, and a serious misunderstanding of what it means to be a Catholic.

The primary and most obvious reason for that is that revelation is not over, *God is constantly revealing himself to us in our experience.* The person of faith cannot ignore experience because his or her religious education has made it unnecessary. Each of us truly needs experience because it is here that most, though not all, of what faith reveals is available for the "seeing." Christian faith is not a way of knowing things which lie beyond the world of human experience. It is rather a way of seeing the deepest reality delivered to us in and by human experience.

But it should immediately be added that personal experiences are not in themselves trustworthy and a sufficient basis for religious conviction. They may be simply the idiosyncratic experiences of one person, who may well be a religious or irreligious fanatic. In order to invest personal experiences with revelatory trustworthiness they must be *communally funded.* This means that they must be reflected on and shared with a community of others who must accept or reject them on the basis of their own personal experiences. So, although personal experience is the initial norm we all use in judging what we read and hear, it is not the ultimate norm. The ultimate and authoritative norm is a whole set of human experiences that are communally funded and that stand the test of public inspection and time. Thus our critical evaluation of the spoken and written word begins with *personal* experience and ends in a *communal* one. *Whatever cannot measure up to this test for validity and trustworthiness can be safely discarded.* To circumvent one's lived experiences in the name of orthodoxy is a serious mistake, since it is in them, and *in them alone* that God is revealed to us.

Obviously, the role of human experience in matters of faith is a issue of the greatest importance. This is because much of what we take to be "traditional" Catholicism is at stake, *e.g.*, the nature of ecclesial authority, the meaning of revelation, the role of the Bible in Christian life, to mention only a few. And since so much is at stake, I fear that it will be some time before the official church succumbs to the inevitable, and claims, as usual, that it has been teaching it all along.

The Pope

In matters of faith, Catholics have two main "authorities" to which they have recourse, the pope and the Bible. But because the Bible is the common heritage of all Christians, the peculiarly "Catholic" source of authority is the pope, and his subordinates the bishops, and their subordinates the local pastors and parish priests. At times boon, at times burden, this traditional hierarchical authority structure is being tested and questioned as never before. Of course, in every institution there has to be someone in charge. But this is so true as to be trivial. The problem is not whether there should be someone in charge, the problem is *how* that charge is carried out. Judgment on the suitability of the manner in which such a charge is carried out is done in the light of why one thinks we have church in the first place.

If we assume that it is for salvation reasons, we get a pretty good idea of how popes came to be viewed as ultimate authorities, and protectors of orthodoxy. For a long time it was thought that salvation goes only to those who not only do it right *(orthopraxis)* but also believe correctly *(orthodoxy)*, and since traditional wisdom stated that it was the job of the church to protect both right-doing and right-believing, popes had their job cut out for them. Their job was made a little easier when, after eighteen hundred years, Vatican I defined the doctrine of papal infallibility. A masterful move, because people worried about salvation could take great hope from knowing that it was now officially guaranteed that their leader had it right. Not an insignificant benefit when one considers what sorts of things the Catholic discipline of the past asked of believers.

Of course, as one comes to think of salvation in categories other than those of *orthopraxis* and *orthodoxy*, one begins to question whether the traditional understanding of papal authority is really right-headed after all. Perhaps God had something else in mind for popes. Perhaps they were called, as Vicars of Christ, to be "present" to the world the way Jesus was. No more. No less. And if this is so, then I think we can better understand the success of John XXIII as pope. Pope-ing, like being a Christian, is primarily an exercise in salvific presence. More than that, we might go so far as to say that whatever authority popes actually come to have in the concrete, stems more from their presence than from their office.

It is a part of traditional theology that the pope can proclaim authoritatively only what the church believes. A classic example of this was the last dogmatic definition of doctrine proclaimed by the church of Rome, the doctrine of the Assumption. Pius XII polled all the bishops and abbots of the world and asked them to poll their people to see if they believed that Mary was assumed bodily into heaven. If the Catholic people already believed it, *then* Pius XII would define it as Catholic dogma. *This* is the classical model of how it works, or at least how it *should* work. Popes are not at liberty to impose anything they like on the Catholic community. Their authority is not over above or over against the *sensus fidelium*; it emerges out of it. Authority is not *had* by them so much as it is *given* to them by the community. And a classic example of what happens when this truth is ignored is Paul VI's encyclical letter on birth control, *Humanae Vitae*. If ever there was a magisterial document stubbornly produced in the face of overwhelming contradictory evidence from faith-filled experience, this is it. As a consequence, it is not viewed as truly authoritative by the majority of Catholics across the world, and is therefore generally ignored. Such is the fate in store for all magisterial teaching that willfully contradicts the *sensus fidelium*.

It is certainly true that the pope is supposed to be the symbol of the unity not only of Christian faith, but of the unity of God with *all* of humankind as well (as John Paul II did so admirably on the day of prayer for peace held at Assisi). This does not mean that the pope is to proclaim something by edict and then effect acceptance by sanction. Unity is not uniformity. The unity to which a pope is called to give witness to the unity amid diversity that the incarnate God of faith is effecting among believers, and in the human community at large.

So in the end, papal authority too is based on the communally funded experiences of humankind. I do not mean to suggest that popes are to be held hostage to some sort of Gallup poll, or that the institutional church is a democratic institution which should be run along the lines of a town hall meeting. Far from it. Nor is the experience on which I see papal authority based the surface or superficial experiences of everyday life, though I don't preclude their also being revelatory. Such experiences underscore the division and cultural diversity of human beings. I am speaking of those deep experiences that flow from our common humanity, from our deepest parts where God dwells. Whenever popes have touched these common human experiences and have witnessed to the unity that they both reveal and effect, their pope-ing has been gift, and their authority the greatest. When they pursue a more parochial path, limiting their concern to intra-church matters, their authority is diminished, and the papacy trivialized.

The Bible

When it comes to the authority question, we find that the Bible gives us two somewhat contradictory accounts. For we read in Matthew 16:18-19:

> Thou art Peter, and upon this Rock I will build my church and the gates of hell shall not prevail against it. And I give to you the keys to the kingdom of heaven. Whatsoever you bind on earth is bound also in heaven, and whatsoever you loose on earth is loosed also in heaven.

But just four chapters later we also read in Matthew 20:24-28:

> Then Jesus called his disciples to him and said: "You know how among the gentiles those in authority lord it over their subordinates and make their authority felt.

> This is not to happen among you. No, he who wants to be great among you must become the servant of all, and he who would be first among you must become the slave of all."

Now which is it? Are those in authority supposed to rule and govern, or are they supposed to serve? The answer, of course, is that you must decide the question of authority as you must every other, not by reference to the book, which in this case is contradictory, but by reference to what the God of faith is revealing in your own life. If you take church authority to be of the ruling kind, know that you have *chosen* to interpret Scripture that way, but you are under no obligation to do so. Nor are those who choose the other view any less Christian or Catholic for doing so.

Such contradictory accounts abound in the Scriptures, and this presents a real problem for those who see the Bible as the Word of God. The Word of God cannot be contradictory. Precisely, but that is why it makes more sense to say that the Bible is not of itself the Word of God, it is primarily a "human" word in response to the presence of God in the lived experiences of a people. But the Bible is not the Qur'an. It is not an eternal and absolute message from God. It is rather the historically dated account and testimony of human beings in particular circumstances regarding the presence of the timeless God in their own lives and in the person of Jesus. The Bible, therefore, cannot be primary, because it is itself a derived book, derived from the life experiences of believers who wrote it down as their testimony of faith for their children and for all believers who came after them.

Of course, the Bible is divinely inspired. Of course, the Bible is divine revelation—no one denies that. *But so is life*! It is precisely because God is present to life and available to human experience that we have a divinely inspired story to tell, and that the story once told is revelation.

It becomes clear, then, that both authority sources, the pope and the Bible, have a derived authority, not indeed from a God in some far-off heaven, but from the God of faith who has pledged to live out life in our presence. This translates into the fact that it is God-filled experience that undergirds both the book and the papacy. Since that is the case, it is wrong-headed to attempt to use either authority source as a way to curb or control the work of the Spirit in and among the people.

The Authority Issue

Any discussion of authority by Catholics must take place against a backdrop of the major division growing between Catholics who invest God's primary authority in life, and those who invest that authority in the Bible, the church, the magisterium, or the pope. There is agreement on both sides that it is God who exercises primary authority in the life of all, believer and non-believer alike. On that point there is no disagreement. The disagreement is rather over in what human institutions or persons authority resides, over the scope and range or field of competence of authority once invested in humans, and over how divine authority is manifested to us humans in this life.

Contrary to what many think, Vatican II did not create this division, but it did exacerbate it and bring it to the forefront in our days. The rise of fundamentalism has put the issue at the center of our consciousness, and raised the question of possible schism. How can both sides co-exist in the same Catholic church? Some have suggested that those who do not accept the authority of the pope, of the church, or of the Bible *as primary* are really Protestants masquerading as Catholics and should leave the church. Certainly, it would be more comfortable if all Catholics agreed on the authority issue, but this is not the case, and it does little good to insist on uniformity on the authority issue just because the authority, which is being questioned, insists on it.

I cannot speak for others, but for myself I want to say that I am a Catholic. I have no intention of leaving, and even less intention of remaining silent on important issues, such as that of papal authority. This does not mean that I am either in open defiance or schismatic, but rather that I am practicing that faithful dissent which has a long tradition in the church. Conservative and fundamentalist Catholics do not have the exclusive Catholic franchise. They, and those who give ear to their pleas for absolute uniformity, are going to have to learn to distinguish between a dissent that destroys and rends the fabric of the believing community and *faithful dissent*.

Authority: As We First Came to Know It

As with so many of life's great truths, we come to know them in a skewered form because as children we just couldn't understand them in their total richness. To the child "authority" is simply "the power to coerce." Parents *have* it, teachers *have* it, policemen *have* it, the bully on the block *has* it, in fact when you're young, it seems authority is what "everyone else" *has*.

As one gets older one makes the distinction between "authority" and "power," and comes to understand that not every use of coercive power is legitimate, *i.e.*, authorized. Authority is then seen as having to do only with the exercise of *legitimate* power, that is, exercising only that power and coercion one has a right to. Authority is legitimate, then, only when it is grounded in some sort of *lex* or law, some set of institutionalized rules. And so we come to understand that our parents derive their authority over us because of the traditional institutions of marriage and family, the police officer derives authority from the duly authorized government, and so it goes.

Having become accustomed to think of authority in these coercive terms, people had no difficulty at all in accepting the notion that in the institution called the Catholic church there had to be, as there must in every institution, a legitimate authority, an authorized coercive force. So it was that the Catholic church began to be seen in much the same way as legitmated authority in the secular order—more and more, being a Catholic prior to Vatican II was identified with obeying the rules and reverencing those in authority to the point that dissent was not tolerated and the total uniformity that was expected was, for the most part, given.

Vatican II changed all this publicly, but even before the Council it was apparent to many that something was wrong with this understanding of authority. Life revealed the God of faith to people, and in the light of this revelation, some just couldn't believe the accepted view on authority. The climate was not conducive to dissent, so many people remained silent. But sometimes, in the sanctity of their own homes, they gave voice to their dissent, and each of us has someone in our own families, a father, a mother, an aunt, or an uncle who was something of a black sheep for saying, in private then, what growing numbers of us are saying, in public now, after Vatican II. *We* are now those mothers, fathers, aunts or uncles, and what we say makes a profound impression on the young who happen to hear us. What are we now saying about church authority in private? What *should* we be saying in the name of God?

Authority: As We Now Understand It

On this sensitive issue, let me not presume to talk in anyone's name but my own, leaving it to the faith community at large to judge the value of what I say.

First of all, authority and coercive power are not the same thing. And what passes for authority in other spheres fails as authority in the realm of faith.

Secondly, not all authority is legitimated, *i.e.*, grounded in the laws and traditions of people. Were this not the case, then it would be hard to explain the obvious authority of the ancient prophets of Israel, of Jesus of Nazareth himself, and in more recent times of a Mohandas Gandhi, a Martin Luther King, Jr., and a John XXIII. Let us call this sort of authority the authority of "gift" or "charism." Not only is this kind of authority not legitimated by law and tradition, it most often witnesses against both, as we see in the case of our contemporary prophets of peace, justice, and sanctuary for Central American refugees.

Thirdly, life eventually teaches that legitimated authority does not extend to the internal forum and applies only to the external "institutional relationships" in which people within an institution find themselves. Put more bluntly, whenever such authority moves into the realm of telling people what to believe and what to think it is no longer competent.

Recently, I was asked why people should believe me rather than the pope on moral matters. That's a legitimate question. Why should you believe me rather than Pope John Paul II? The only answer I can give you is that you shouldn't, that is, you shouldn't *unless* your own life experience more nearly corroborates what I say than what he says. In short, you shouldn't unless you want to and by so doing are better able to make sense of your life as a believer, the obvious implication being that should your faith-experience not jibe with what authorities are saying, you *must* look elsewhere.

In this matter of faith, authority is not "had" by virtue of office—it is "given" by virtue of presence. So in regard to faith authorities, I would say: Who are the people who by their presence, not merely their words, speak the Kingdom to you? They are your faith authorities, follow them. And in the end, this is the way our pope's get their faith-authority too. And that is why the most powerful and authoritative pope the world has known was John XXIII. Protestants, those of other religions, even atheists *gave* him that authority—just as people did with Jesus 2000 years ago.

Those who dwell in, or regularly frequent, their deepest humanity, the realm of incarnate spirit, should have no difficulty recognizing their own experiences in my account of authority. But this will surely not come as "good news" to fundamentalist minds, whose passion for certainty and order will not allow them to see a difference between authority over externals in the secular order and authority in the internal realm of the spirit. Nor will it be acceptable to those who refuse to grow up and take responsibility for what they *become,* preferring to be told what to *do,* thereby insuring their salvation.

Of course, salvation no longer means what we thought it did, so perhaps we had better consider the effect of our theology of presence on the traditional view of salvation next.

CHAPTER FOUR

SALVATION FOR INCARNATE SPIRITS

There is definitely something "fishy" about the traditional view of "salvation" among Catholics. Vatican II made this clear, and now we are in the process of rethinking all of our theology. We have done quite well with things like the liturgy, what we think about church, the importance of the ministry of all the faithful, etc., but there are two areas, especially, where we remain pre-Vatican II. One of them is our understanding of sacraments, although there has been some encouraging movement toward a more enlightened view in this area in the past few years. The other is an area where we remain absolutely primitive, *i.e.,* our understanding of salvation. We have just begun to re-thematize our notion of "salvation." Those who attempt it are certain to be met with anger and frustration from their fellow Catholics, because in the end "being saved" is what religion is really all about. Indeed, many only remain in the church because they feel that by so doing, they are better insuring their salvation.

The Traditional View of Salvation

What, you ask, is so "fishy" about the traditional view of salvation? There are so many things that should have given us a clue that we were on the wrong track that it is hard to know where to begin. First of all, it is so hopelessly self-centered. It means "having all *my* needs met," complete and total satisfaction, complete and total *personal* happiness. And to achieve this bonanza, all I must do is be sure that I "die in the state of grace." There is really nothing "communal" or holistic about such a view. It makes salvation not only very individualistic, but something not of *this* world, something to be achieved in the next life, in that infamous "other" world. A truly impoverished view. As if our world were the first stage of a multi-staged rocket, and totally expendable. As if this beautiful world of ours, so filled with and loved by God, the theater of our earthly lives, is to be discarded and destroyed by God after human beings have worked out their eternal salvation here. *Nothing could be further from the truth,* if we but remember God's dream of transforming *this* world into the Kingdom. How could we have forgotten?

It is our Platonic heritage, again, that plays a key role in our forgetting our Jewish roots. Viewing matter as a hindrance to spirit, misunderstanding the role of the human body in the work of spirit, we could not help but also misunderstand the role and significance of the material world in the economy of salvation. Burdened as we so often are by body and the material world, we just naturally fell into thinking about salvation in terms of escaping both our bodies and the world. We get a much better "fit" with a notion of salvation that involves not only the transformation of our inner world and attitudes, but also the transformation of the outer world in which we live. It is inconceivable that we should have thought we could come to personal fulfillment all the while leaving our world behind—a world disintegrated and divided by hatred, passion, domination, greed and injustice. As we have now come to understand, that would not be "salvation" at all, but its very antithesis.

But our willingness to accept an "other-worldly" view of salvation stems from another source as well, a secular source that was only to happy to re-enforce the over-spiritualized views of the Christian churches, *i.e.,* Western secular culture. The individualistic, one-sided, over spiritualized view of salvation was inculcated into us from two sides then, the church and the "State." Put bluntly, Western industrialized states have a vested interest in keeping Christians looking for salvation in some other world and some other time. It relieves government-directed pressures that would otherwise arise to transform *this* world into a place more suited to *human* habitation, thus witnessing the presence of God.

Arising out of the Industrial Revolution, the modern Western secular state has adopted the same compartmentalization (which made mass production so effective) as its societal model. Our very language tells the story. We speak of the "secular" state, which means it is a domain other than and over against anything religious. The traditional American doctrine of "separation of church and State" is just the natural outcome of compartmentalization. Before the Industrial Revolution, life for many was less compartmentalized and more holistic. Faith and religion were often accepted to be at the center of things. But with the breakdown of such a unified view of life, faith and religion were set apart from the other dimensions of life. Using the efficiency model, it was easy to justify such developments, since clearly the churches were concerned with "salvation" which had nothing to do with *this* world or *this* time, but were concerned with the "other" world and eternity. To facilitate the churches doing their salvific work, it was best to keep them out of the center of things, where politics, economics and business reigned supreme. More than that, as things developed the churches were only tolerated as long as they didn't make any pretensions to be concerned with domains beyond the one assigned to them by the secular state, *i.e.,* the totally private enterprise of saving individual souls.

At first sight, the modern Western democracies seem to be benefactors to religious people because they staunchly defend the principle of religious liberty. But on closer inspection, what that really means is that people are at liberty to believe what they please, *so long as what they believe has no impact on the world in which they live.* Religion/faith is to be a strictly private affair. The vicissitudes of contemporary industrial living take a real human toll, so a second task assigned to the churches by the secular state has been to extend a place where those who are "beaten up" by the system can have an experience of real community. Sure the world is a tough place, and people get hurt, but there are always the churches on the sidelines offering the wounded solace. No need to attempt to change the world into a better place, for experiences of community are available to all who want them, available in the churches. That's their job, to make such experiences available to contemporary women and men so that they will not become totally discontent with the reality of their lives here, but will yearn for a better day in the hereafter. When the churches, in appreciation for the secular culture's proclamation of religious freedom, meekly accept the two tasks assigned to them by the secular state, they of course become sorely compromised, *integrated* into the system, and unable to proclaim and witness the really Good News. Their members become inoculated with just enough Christianity to be immune to the real thing.

The irony of it all, of course, is that in the name of religious freedom and an "other-worldly" salvation the Christian churches of Western societies have been compartmentalized, trivialized, and privatized so as to be all but impotent to affect public policy. If this is the outcome of the traditional view of salvation, perhaps it really is time to tell a different, but not necessarily a brand new, "salvation" story.

Salvation and Ancient Israel

In its venerable history, Israel also went through a similar process of "spiritualization" in its notion of salvation, and for much the same reasons as those given above. By the time of Christ the apocalyptic literature, influenced by the Greek notion of individual immortality, had, in turn, influenced Jews to look for a personal salvation "out of this world," much the same as the majority of Christians do today. But this was *not* their deepest tradition, any more than it is ours.

Originally, the Hebrews had a much more down-to-earth, if not earthy, notion of salvation. We can see it expressed in Psalm 144:12–15:

> That our sons may grow up as the young plants and that our daughters may be as the polished corner of the Temple. That our garners may be full and plenteous with all manner of stores; that our sheep may bring forth thousands and ten thousands in our streets; that our oxen may be strong to labor; that there be no leading into captivity, and no complaining in our streets. Happy are the people that are in such a state. Blessed are the people who have the Lord for their God.

Some might want to call such a view of salvation "materialistic," but it is perhaps more appropriate to say it is comprehensive and wide-ranging. To its credit, it is not Platonic and other worldly. Biological, familial, psychological, economic, social, and political needs are all mentioned. The Bible is consistent in this regard. Throughout it we find salvation spoken of in terms of food, happiness, peace, and justice. But even though salvation can never be divorced from human well-being for the ancient Hebrews, it cannot be equated with it either. No matter how prosperous and fortunate, no matter how well integrated familially and socially, the blessings of life and of the earth are gifts of Yahweh, the Creator-God, the God of Exodus and the covenant. They are no more than this, and to treat them as more is idolatry. So the psalmist adds to the litany of desired blessings the greatest blessing of all: "Blessed are the people who have the Lord for their God."

The psalmist's hope of an intense personal, individual, and very concrete and earthy salvation exists within the framework of the covenant between God, the Lord of salvation, and the people of God. Originally, before the Greek influence, it would have been unthinkable for Israel to think of salvation solely in terms of private, individual happiness. It was impossible to seek the God of the covenant by or for oneself. To seek God and God's salvation was necessarily to seek it for one's fellow humans, and ultimately for the whole world. And what was saved and salvaged was not a one-dimensional "spiritual" life, but a full and fully *human* life, that is to say, a life incarnate, relational, physical, psychological, and spiritual.

But the covenant did not guarantee salvation, that is to say, it did not guarantee that life would become as the psalmist described. For that to happen, Israel had to observe the laws, which were not primarily dietary at all, but were social, concerned primarily with human relationships (cf. Leviticus 26:3-13). Human well-being in this life was dependent on Israel's keeping the covenant observance, which was the proper treatment of all in the community, with special emphasis on caring for and not exploiting the poor and disadvantaged. This observance marked a godly people, the People of God, and made Yahweh bless them and made Yahweh's face to shine on them. Sin, in this fundamental Hebrew account, was enslaving others, causing or extending poverty, closing one's heart to strangers and the needy, in short, seeking salvific well-being merely for oneself. Doing this was to break covenant with Yahweh and to not "...have the Lord as your God."

Since the Law (Torah) contained exhortations and prohibitions regarding these things, it was easy to come to think of sin simply as breaking the law. Later, some members of Israel were to succumb to the temptation, but many continued to remember the significance of Exodus and the covenant and to view sin as the skewering of the proper relations God called them to, both with one another and with Yahweh.

Experience, too, corroborated Israel's best instincts regarding sin and salvation. Their experience of pain, suffering, fighting for survival as a people, and their experience of alienation all revealed both what sin really is, and in what the salvation offered by Yahweh consisted. To enslave, to exploit, to dominate—all cause the divisions and alienations in humankind to spread like cancer. We generally think of Genesis as giving us an account of the fall, but it does much more than that. From the primal fall, there follows a whole series of "falls," each widening the circle of alienation and division, culminating in the Tower of Babel story:

> Adam and Eve - Genesis 2-3
> Cain and Abel - Genesis 4:1-16
> Patriarch Lemech - Genesis 4:23-24
> Noah and the Flood - Genesis 6:6-7

Noah and His Family - Genesis 9:18-27
The Tower of Babel - Genesis 11:1-9

Israel well understood and chronicled the fact that sin unchecked brings about the total disintegration of human life. (Ancient Israel would well understand the malaise of our nuclear age.) Alphonse Spilly suggests that we have given so much attention to the fall of Adam and Eve that we have missed a basic insight of Genesis, which is that sin has devastating effects *on the quality of life among humans on this earth,* and that consequently *the quality of human life on this earth is integral to any notion of salvation.*[11]

In my judgment, *this* is the deepest and most venerable tradition of both Jews and Christians, and is why Vatican II's call for us to better live the *social* dimension of the Gospel and of salvation is not a new call at all. It is a *radical* call, in the sense that it calls us to return to the deepest "roots" of our faith. Those who reject Vatican II because they think it is too innovative, feel this way because they take the integrated, privatized, and trivialized version of Christianity from the recent past to be normative and traditional. It clearly is not.

Salvation in the biblical sense cannot be understood one-dimensionally, in narrow, reductionist, parochial ways. The salvation the Scriptures speak of offers a comprehensive wholeness in this fragmented and alienated life. Salvation in the biblical sense is a newness of life, the unfolding of true humanity in the fullness of God (Colossians 2:9), it is salvation of the soul and the body, of the individual and society, of humankind and the whole of creation (Romans 8:19). So, if we are to be true to our "deepest" tradition, our witness to salvation must be *comprehensive, holistic,* and as we shall see, *ecumenical.* Salvation can never arise out of parochialism or sectarianism precisely because these are the very sorts of things our "deepest" tradition calls sin and from which God wishes to liberate and save us.

The Indeterminateness of the Early Christian View

When it came to understanding the meaning of the life and death of Jesus, the first Christians were blessed with a wealth of possible interpretations. This, no doubt, accounts for the fact that the Christian understanding of salvation remained much more open-ended than other central doctrines of faith, *e.g.*, the Trinity, the Incarnation, etc. This remains true today, since Christians are still able to interpret the life, death, and resurrection of Jesus in manifold ways. But whichever of the possible understandings of salvation one adopts, it must be rooted in and integrated around some common central New Testament message. St. Paul seems to present that central core when he says:

> All this has been done by God, who has reconciled us to himself through Christ and has given us the ministry of reconciliation. I mean that God, in Christ, was reconciling the world to himself, not counting humankind's transgressions against them, and that he has entrusted the message of reconciliation to us. This makes us ambassadors for Christ, God as it were appealing through us. (2 Corinthians 5:18-20)

Some may prefer to find the centrality of the Christian Scriptures elsewhere, but it strikes me that all the other essential elements of Christian faith are well integrated in and manifestations of the fact that salvation *is* reconciliation.

The New Testament leaves no doubt as to just who the agent of salvation/reconciliation is, *i.e.*, God, or God in Christ. Nor is there any doubt as to who is reconciled to whom. God is not reconciled, nor does God reconcile the Godhead to the world; rather we, and our world, are reconciled to God. But the fact that we are the recipients of this salvific activity on the part of God in Christ Jesus, does not at all mean that we are merely passive in the work of salvation/reconciliation. Not at all. Paul clearly says that having been reconciled, we are by that very fact enlisted in a "ministry of reconciliation," and are called to be "ambassadors for Christ," which means that in our very person we are to become God's own appeal to others for reconciliation.

Now it is all too easy, as we have seen, to interpret this solely in spiritual terms of our relationship with God and with one another. But more is involved than the transformation of our inner space, important though that may be. For Paul does not say that God was reconciling humankind to God, though this is the way the passage is most often interpreted. No. He says that God was, in Christ, reconciling the whole world. Reconciliation in Christ is to effect some sort of transformation of the real world of everyday life, the world of incarnate spirits. Only if so understood can the notion of reconciliation be foundational for the other essential elements of our faith, such as love of neighbor, peace, justice, and the coming Kingdom.

Of course, this means that commitment to change and transform the human world in which we live cannot be regarded as optional, or a matter of individual choice for Christians. In the more recent past, it was generally felt that those who concerned themselves with social issues such as war, nuclear weapons, women's rights, fair employment and the like, and did so in the name of God, were really religious fanatics. Here, too, Vatican II has changed all this. We now see that we were wrong headed with our privatized and trivialized Christianity, and that transforming this world into the Kingdom must become a top priority for us. It always should have been. Christian faith is not an enterprise to prepare us for some other world, that "other" world and our salvation will take care of themselves if we but take care of our "ministry of reconciliation" to *this* world. That reconciliation "of the world" was the goal of Christ's entire life, and those who claim to follow in his footsteps are called to a "ministry of reconciliation," as St. Paul said. Perhaps as we approach the third millennium of Christian faith, it might just be about time to start focusing in on the central issue. Reconciliation in our human world means that our calling and ministry is to establish peace. This task is a quite concrete one and it means that *the Christian community must become a place of peace, a saving place.*

Understanding the Murder of Jesus

If one accepts this high-sounding talk about reconciliation as *the* central element in Christianity, one must still make some sort of sense out of the brutal murder of Jesus. We too often use euphemisms to speak of it, talking about his "death," his "crucifixion," or his "sacrifice," referring to the whole bloody mess as the "Paschal Mystery." But by any objective account, we would have to say that Jesus was tortured and then murdered. How are we to make sense of such brutality at the heart of God's work of reconciliation?

This remains troublesome and no account of salvation can possibly avoid speaking to it. The first Christians, too, were unable to avoid it, and so they searched their souls and their tradition to see how, in the light of their experience of God and Jesus as "present" to them, to make sense of Jesus' bloody end.

Leaning heavily on the rich and varied traditions of Israel, they couched their understandings in the familiar language of Old Testament cultic sacrifice. Strangely enough, though the Old Testament is replete with talk of sacrifices and the regulations governing them, there is little or nothing explicitly said about the theology, or meaning, of sacrifice. Either everyone "knew" what they meant and so there was no need to write it down, or perhaps the exact meaning was left to each offerer of sacrifice in her or his relations with Yahweh. Here again we see a certain open-mindedness about such things. Great specificity about the rules for performing the sacrificial rites, great variety and openness in the understanding of them. In any event, it is difficult for us some three millennia later, and after almost two millennia of Christian misunderstanding, to recapture the real meaning behind the blood offerings of the Old Testament. But the early Christians used those varied meanings to fashion their own understanding of Jesus' work of reconciliation.

To ancient people the breath was the principal life-source, but the blood and the heart were the physical locus of that life-source in the body. Life was dynamic and the flowing blood was the vehicle of that life. Blood offerings, then, were much more symbolic of life than of death to the ancient mind. So in their sacrificial rites, the ancient Hebrews would pour the blood on the ground, would smear it on the horns of the altar, and even on the veil in the Holy of Holies. Blood was seen to be life-giving. So it was not at all necessary to interpret all blood offerings as retribution for sin and guilt, one could choose to see them that way, but there were more positive perspectives possible as well.

The sacrifices of ancient Israel were primarily of four main types. The first three were "bloody" sacrifices involving the killing of animals. *Holocausts* were the most solemn, in which the offering was totally consumed, and not shared in by priest, people, or offerer. These were very special acts of consecration showing Yahweh's total dominion. There were the *peace offerings* in thanksgiving, in relation to some vow or promise, and free-will offerings. In these only part of the offering was destroyed, and often the family making the offering would be given part of it to have a "feast before the Lord." Then there were the *sacrifices of atonement*, offered to expiate for sin and guilt. Finally, there was a fourth offering, of grain, which usually accompanied one of the other three. Now in this context, it was easy for the first Christians to see Jesus' bloody end as similar to each of the bloody sacrifices of the Old Law. Somehow, Jesus was a holocaust, a peace offering, but most significantly a sacrifice of atonement.

To anyone familiar with Isaiah, Jesus' life and suffering could not help but remind them of the "Suffering Servant of the Lord" as described in Servant oracles in Chapters 42 to 53. Jesus is seen as having vicariously suffered for the People of God, as described in Isaiah. In this account, Jesus' bloody end is a sign and guarantee that he is indeed the "Servant of the Lord."

But the suffering servant motif of Isaiah gave rise to another understanding. Jesus is our "scapegoat," as it were. His suffering is seen as "penal suffering," in the sense that he took on the sins and iniquities of the whole human race, and was willing to accept the punishment for us all. This restores right order, since the sins of the people were expiated by the suffering of the innocent Jesus.

A similar and alternative understanding arose that stressed not so much the fact that Jesus took on human iniquity and therefore was subject to punishment (penal suffering), but rather the free-will dimension of his offering. Jesus, out of love for us, puts up bail, for us as it were. This understanding looked to civil law, and the practice of putting up bond for wrong-doers. Jesus is our bondsman. As such he "redeems" us, which is to say, "buys us back."

Yet another variation of this theme is found in the understanding that by his bloody end, Jesus rescued us from the evil one, salvaged the human race, ransomed the captives, and won the human race for Yahweh as a kind of booty.

Finally, because the early Christians knew Jesus lived, because they could experience his presence in their lives, they interpreted his bloody offering of himself as the new "passover," the new Exodus to freedom, the Paschal Mystery leading to a "new" creation and the Coming Kingdom.

Clearly, all of these "understandings" are important to what the New Testament authors are trying to say about the meaning of Jesus' life and death. But equally clear is the fact that no one of these "understandings" can be taken as definitive or normative. They all contribute something to our understanding of how Jesus did the great work of reconciliation.

But on so important a matter as salvation we humans are not comfortable with a diversity of understandings, so we tend to zero in on one of them and make it normative. And so it was that from this rich multiplicity of understandings that the Christian church zeroed in on the one that viewed Jesus' life and death as a work of atonement or expiation for our sins. But here again the indeterminateness of the basic issue reasserted itself, this time in the Christian context, and gave rise to three typically Christian views of atonement, with a wide variety of interpretation of detail within each type.

Three Christian Theories of Atonement

The first is the *classical* theory, which was originally formulated by the Greek Fathers, and which was the heart of Luther's radical reformation view. The second, more familiar to Catholics, is the *Latin* theory. Inspired by Tertullian and first proposed by Cyprian, it was given its most complete expression by St. Anselm. Basically inspired by Roman law, it was so powerfully and coherently articulated by Anselm that it became the traditional Catholic view in the minds of many. And the third view, which is the prevailing view in our day, is not so much concerned with the objective order of atonement, but rather with the "subjective" effects of Christ's work of reconciliation on the individual person. Peter Abelard seems to have been advocating this sort of understanding, and at about the same time as Anselm was advocating his. We might call this the *subjective* theory, not meaning that it is merely subjective, not at all, but rather that its primary focus is not the objective order of sin, guilt, and restitution of right order, but rather the transformation of the total human subject.

The Classical Theory of the Greek Fathers

According to this view, the world, the theater of human life and action, is alienated and divided, subject to darkness and death, and is in the evil grip of the devil. As long as these powers dominate the world the human race will remain imprisoned, enslaved to sin, subject to the darkness of death and evil, and even subject to the wrath of God. There can be no liberation from this situation from within the world, since all potential liberators from within the world are themselves enslaved. It is a vicious (literally, evil and vice-laden) circle. If reconciliation of the world is to occur, it requires someone to do battle against the forces of darkness which control and dominate our world, to break the vicious circle. This can only be done by an "outsider," someone not enslaved and subject to the forces of darkness. Left to itself, humankind is doomed, because the only *real* "outsider," obviously, is God.

According to the classical theory's understanding of the New Testament, that is exactly what happened in Jesus. In him, we have God's own loving "exodus toward" humankind. God's journey to the far country involved a life-death struggle with the forces of darkness, and it cost Jesus his life. He was murdered, dying on a cross, but that cross is the ultimate sign of God's victory over all the forces of darkness: sin, death, and the evil one. The sinless one overcame them all and was raised in glory, thus altering the basic constitution of the world, redeeming and liberating humankind, making it possible for us to make an "exodus toward" God, *i.e.,* toward reconciliation, life, and goodness. God's intervention was a real revolution, changing the basic order of things, initiating the exodus of the whole human race toward the Kingdom.

This rather primitive understanding of salvation/reconciliation could not prevail forever—it makes salvation/reconciliation too mechanical, too automatic, and quite impersonal. The human race seems to be little more than the bone of contention between God and the forces of darkness and evil. Still, there are many Christians, especially more fundamentalist types, who continue in our day to espouse this primitive view. The problem is that they stress the negative dimensions of it, rather than the positive, of which there are many. So certain elements of this view remain important and essential to Christians even in our day.

First of all, it is "realistic" about the human condition. The human race is sorely divided and alienated, but this is not on account of fate or the original constitution of reality; rather it is the direct result of sin. (Recall the Genesis account of how alienation spreads due to human agency.) All of which stresses another important element in the classical view, namely that human beings are connected and bonded to one another, sharing not only a common world but a common destiny. Salvation or reconciliation is not primarily for individuals, but for all of humankind.

Secondly, and more importantly, though it is not stressed in this view, reconciliation is God's idea. God did not wait on conditions; there are no strings attached to the salvation or reconciliation offered, it is given gratuitously and unconditionally out of love. For the church Fathers, God's sovereignty is one of love, God does not leave humankind to stew in its own juices, but initiates salvation/reconciliation in our behalf, *for us*. There is a close connection in this theory between salvation/ reconciliation and human liberation. What is at stake is the salvaging of human's total life, temporal and eternal. It involves the "exodus toward" life of all creation. In terms of its positive elements the *classical* theory is not only *not* primitive, it is wonderfully perennial.

The Roman Law Theory of Atonement

There is a shift from the cosmic order of things as expressed in the classical view, to the more mundane and practical order of the law. Tertullian was struck by the absurdity of forgiveness without penance and restitution. This just didn't seem right. You either make satisfaction, or you pay the penalty, that was the proper "legal" way of doing things. So it was that Jesus' suffering and death came to be seen as *compensatory satisfaction* for the sins of humankind. Someone had to make satisfaction. We humans were incapable of doing so, so God did it for us in Christ Jesus. And since satisfaction was made, no further penalty need be imposed. Humankind is *saved*.

This no-nonsense, very legalistic, anthropomorphic, view of the situation became normative for the Roman church largely due to the systematic account given of it by Anselm of Canterbury. Attempting to understand why God became incarnate in Jesus, Anselm reasoned as follows:

> Insult and injury are judged not by the status or dignity of the one committing the injury but rather by the status or dignity of the one sustaining it. This makes sin some-

thing human beings can do, but not undo. As an offense against God, there is no way a mere human being can give adequate satisfaction to God for the injury and insult sustained by the sin. Now God could have settled for imperfect or less than adequate satisfaction, and let it go at that. But then human beings would be under a cloud, as it were, never having their sins and transgression fully satisfied.

Given this scenario, there was only one way to fully right the situation. A divine person/being would have to make satisfaction for it to be adequate, but in order for it to be proper as well, the one making satisfaction should also be human, because it was humankind's sins that tendered the insult in the first place. By reflecting on such things, Anselm thought he had discovered why it was that God *had* to become incarnate in order to save humankind from sin. Only one who was both God and human could do what was required, and Jesus was that one.

The Latin theory moves with impeccable logic. It is legally precise and correct, but for all its brilliance it seems to leave little place for love, which was the greatest asset of the classical view. Amid all the search for intellectual understanding, reconciliation/salvation seems to have lost its human face. Love seems to enter, if at all, only tangentially. As a result, this view never deserved to become the dominant one, and the fact is that Peter Abelard was taking an entirely different tack and was doing so in Anselm's own lifetime.

Still, in fairness to Anselm, God's dignity and honor were never conceived by him in an egoistic way. God's honor is inextricably woven into relations with the human race. God is honored when peace and justice obtain between God and humankind, and among all the members of the human race.

The Subjective/Humanist View of Atonement

Back in the twelfth century, Peter Abelard's position was the counterpoint of Anselm's. Abelard was not interested in the legalisms of the situation, *i.e.*, sin and its satisfaction, as reasons for God's exodus to the far country of the human race. Rather, his interest lay in trying to understand what the effect of God's physical entrance into humankind in Jesus had on human beings. What was the effect of the atonement, the salvation/

reconciliation, of Jesus on individual human beings? What was the effect of Jesus' "presence" on people? What was the effect of his death?

And always, the answer was the same: *love*. Jesus incarnated the infectious power of God's absolute and unconditional love of humankind. His authority arose from his ability to enkindle love in human hearts. People were delighted to be with him, they felt more human in his presence than they had ever felt before. And their hearts almost burst out of them, so filled with love were they when they contemplated the fact that Jesus was willing to love them, to be for them, even at the cost of his own life. More than the preceding two theories, Abelard brought out the essential elements of the New Testament account of Jesus, and his approach to salvation/reconciliation has a peculiarly modern ring to it. What he said back then is just about what our contemporary theologians are saying today.

But before one simply rejects the preceding theories and makes this subjective view normative, it should be noted that there is something essential missing from Abelard's account. In the enthusiasm to break away from the more objective and legalistic accounts of salvation/reconciliation, whatever happened to "sin" and "alienation"? While it is certainly true that love can conquer those things, and has, it is no less true that they remain harsh and very real realities in our everyday lives. As we come more and more to stress the centrality of love in the work of reconciliation, we must be careful not to make sin a trivial matter. It is all too real.

The Enduring Relevance of All Three Theories

What seems evident in this perusal of the various "understandings" of salvation/reconciliation is that the church never felt obliged to choose among these theories. It did not see the three theories as diametrically opposed or mutually exclusive, but rather as complementary. This means that Christian understanding of the work of reconciliation is relatively open. There is something important to be taken from *each* of the theories, and there is no need to make any one of them normative or obligatory. The very existence of a multiplicity of views guards us against any one-sided reductionism, and should encourage us to be open-minded as we seek an "understanding" of God's salvific presence in our times.

As we do this, we shall find that each of the traditional theories stresses something basic and important, something we ignore at our own peril. So in our contemporary search, the theories continue to act as a kind of guidance. The classical theory witnesses to the absolutely sovereign love of a God who refuses to abandon the world and freely chooses to physically enter it in order to save it. The Latin theory underscores the fact that no matter what sort of an account we give of salvation/reconciliation it must make sense to the human mind. Faith not only seeks, but requires understanding. The subjective theory keeps us mindful that in the end reconciliation requires an inner transformation or conversion on our part, and that we cannot rely on any objective reality, be it icon, practice, or devotion, to guarantee salvation. Salvation has already been guaranteed in and by Jesus, and to avail ourselves of it we need only accept it. But that means becoming infected with the same love he had, and spreading that infection into the everyday world. We need to keep all these things in mind as we seek a contemporary understanding of our faith and of the work of reconciliation.

Salvation: A Psychological Perspective

The number of people availing themselves of the sacrament of reconciliation has been decreasing worldwide, and it is easy to conclude from this that contemporary women and men have lost their sense of sin, and hence their sense of needing salvation. But the numbers involved in some sort of therapy have risen sharply, and so it might be better to suggest that people are seeking salvation elsewhere, rather than that they have no sense of needing it. The fact is, each person cries out for a safe place, a place of caring, of being intact and preserved. The experience of therapists clearly indicates that *each person needs a "place" where the fragments and loose ends of life can be collected, experienced, and treated with care, a place of salvation.* So it isn't so much that contemporary women and men experience no need of "salvation," but rather the need they experience is the very real and concrete need of human well-being which must be met here and now, not hereafter. In that respect, a Platonic Christianity simply will not fill the bill. Of course, a therapy that excludes the blessing of "having the Lord for our God" and remains totally unconcerned about the personal well-being of others won't, as the Judaeo-Christian tradition attests, ultimately be salvific either. But people take salvation wherever they can find it, even if it be only partial, and the fact of the matter is growing numbers of us seem to find some sort of "salvation" in counseling or therapy.

It is in the counseling session, rather than in the churches, that many come to recognize those elements of salvation we have been discussing. Freed temporarily from the burdens of everyday relationships and problems that damage us, fatigue us, and literally wear us down, the counselee, facing a benign and caring presence, has the experience of being in a "safe" or "saving" place. A place of safety wherein it might just be possible to end the fragmentation, to gather up the disparate threads of one's life and weave them together into some sort of meaningful tapestry. It is an exhilarating (and salvific) experience in an otherwise harassing and alienating world. As we saw in an earlier chapter, "presence," as the work of spirit, has a way of working such marvels. No wonder some people don't ever want the therapy to end!

In addition to being etymologically related to "safety," the word "salvation" is also related to "salvage." When you salvage something you not only give it a safe place, you rescue it from harm, you treat it with care, you protect it for the future. The work of salvaging goes on against the ravages of time and the environment, it requires extensive preparation, repeated divings and skillful and painstaking restoration. Those images of salvaging illuminate important dimensions of therapy (and of salvation). Repeated divings into our own depths are required if we are to really know who we are, and come to any significant degree of self-acceptance.

From the psychological point of view, what in our lives is to be salvaged, is to be saved? The answer is *meaning*. In psychological language, salvation refers to the discovery of the meaning in one's life. Salvation as salvaging refers to each person touching the depth of her or his experience and being, and thus discovering the reason for her or his own existence. This puts one in touch with the core of one's life and experience, wherein lies meaning. (We have already discussed why this is so in Chapter Three.)

Most of our days are spent in daily routines, lived out on the surface. We avoid the depths. But then something happens, a crisis, an unexpected gesture of kindness, a look, a word, and for a moment we are stopped in our tracks. Life on the surface recedes, something opens up, we are touched by and and are in touch with "the depths." Without being able to verbalize it, I am exhilarated, vitalized, more fully alive. I sense that there is purpose to my existence, even though I do not grasp its totality. Of course, the exhilaration cannot last. Indeed, in a world freighted by time it cannot last, but we make an abiding mistake if we think such moments are illusory or insignificant. However briefly, the fabric of my life has been torn open and I experience my own depths and feel cherished, at home, whole and safe. And in that same experience I have been able to gaze deeply in the reality of my own humanity and have touched the mystery of the transcendent presence playing through my life. It is in such moments in the depths that we come to recognize and concretely experience salvation. The trick is not to forget what we have learned as we return to life on the surface.

Conclusion

We should not be disturbed at the thought that people find salvation/reconciliation apart from the churches. Indeed, our Christian faith reveals why and how this can happen. Not only are we not to take some rigid, univocal view of salvation, we are not to presume that we can somehow limit God in the work of the Spirit, *the reconciliation of the world to God*. And because we know God to be present to all of humankind, salvation/reconciliation can occur anywhere, anytime, under any circumstances. But the effects and signs of that salvific presence are always the same. People, themselves, become more whole, more loving, and more "able to be truly present to their world and to one another." In short, they are saved and reconciled. And what is more, it happens in *this* life and in *this* world, not in some other life or world. Perhaps the best expression of this is from Parker Palmer:

> To be saved, to be made whole, is to realize that we are in the contradictions, that the contradictions are in us,

> and that all of it is held together by a "hidden wholeness." It is to be able to anywhere with anyone, in freedom and in love. To be whole is to know one's relatedness to all of life, to the dark and the light, the evil and the good, the strange and the familiar. It is to walk freely across the earth knowing that God is with us whether we climb to the heavens or descend into hell. The liberation of the cross is knowing that there is no contradiction which God cannot overcome.[12]

Palmer went on, "You don't think your way into a new kind of living: you live your way into a new kind of thinking." We are not so much called to have a right "understanding" of salvation/reconciliation, as we are called to experience and live it. And it is to the day to day living of it that we now turn.

CHAPTER FIVE

COMMUNITY: THE SAVING PLACE

Everywhere these days, one hears much talk about "community," and yet there is no topic about which there is so much confusion and misunderstanding. In parishes all across North America, pastors and their pastoral teams are urging their people to "form community," and the people ask themselves why all of a sudden there is so much community-talk when they have obviously gotten along very well for so many years without it. People ask, "If community is really all that important, why didn't they say more about it years ago?

Why Suddenly "Community"?

Why suddenly all this stress on community? The reason is simple and direct. Most of us learned that the reason there was church at all was in order to insure the salvation of souls. To that end, parishes were put up in every neighborhood to insure that the seven sacraments, which were said to be the "means to salvation," would be easily available to all. By availing ourselves of the sacraments, and dying in the state of grace, we saved our individual and immortal souls. Given that account of why we have church, there was obviously no reason to talk much about community. Besides, everyone was so busy saving his or her own soul that there wasn't time for community anyway.

The reason for the sudden epidemic of "community talk" is that, thanks to Vatican II, we have a different account not only of why we have church, but also, (as we just saw in the previous chapter), of the meaning of "sin" and "salvation." And as is clear from what has already been said, this does not mean that we are suddenly holding something new. Far from it. We are simply reclaiming something essential from our ancient Judaeo-Christian tradition, something we evidently lost or forgot along the way. For those of us raised in the twentieth century before Vatican II, "sin" was seen as breaking a law or rule that God had established for the human race. But our ancestors in faith, the ancient Hebrews, had an entirely different notion of what "sin" was, and hence of what "salvation" was, too. As we have already seen, the Genesis story clearly told them of the consequences of humankind's not living "relationally," of not living in solidarity with one another, of not really being "present" to one another, and to their world. The dissonance and disharmony of Babel were the consequences. So Israel always had a deep understanding that God's plan was otherwise. The dream of God for humankind, was that they live relationally, in peace, solidarity and redemptive intimacy—thus becoming real signs of God's abiding presence. Human beings are born into families, are born of the intimacy between a man and a woman. Everything about our origins and beginnings bespeaks our ultimate connectedness to one another. We receive the gift of life in relation, and we are to live it relationally and in solidarity with all of humankind.

That's God's plan for us. But as we know all too well, we

have *chosen* to live in alienation and division, and to see our lives as somehow our very own, not a gift to be shared. That's the good old American way of rugged individualism, and yet that's precisely what the ancient Hebrews, our ancestors in faith, understood by sin. The sin that Jesus fought to overcome is precisely that situation which too many of us take to be "normal"—alienation, division, and fragmentation in humankind and in our world. *This* is *the* fundamental sin. It was this sin which moved God to liberate the Jews from Egypt by exodus, it was this sin that caused Yahweh to call Israel to be Yahweh's own "relational" people; it was this sin that was the occasion for raising up the prophets of Israel to call the people back to the dream, it is this sin that Jesus' "work of reconciliation" was meant to eradicate from human hearts so that the Kingdom of God might truly come.

In recapturing the ancient perspective, Vatican II changed everything for us Catholics, and underscored the latent opposition that exists between the dream of God and the American Dream. Since sin is now viewed as a state as well as an act, it is no longer enough for us to see to it that we don't "commit" sins, we now must be careful to examine our lives to see whether we aren't actually "living in" sin. I can keep all of the commandments, and in the old sense be in the "state of grace" and still not be living in faith-filled solidarity with my sisters and brothers, still not be living the dream of God. In short, I can be free of "sins" and thus in the "state of grace," but still be "living in sin" because I have closed my heart to others, will not be "present" to them, and refuse to be reconciled with them.

As we now see, it is not enough to be free of individual "sins." In order to be about the "ministry of reconciliation" we are called to, we must strive also to stop "living in sin." And what is the opposite of "living in sin" from this perspective? Why, "living in community," of course.

That is why we are suddenly besieged not only with talk of "community," but also with talk of "peace and justice," and concern for the poor and disadvantaged. These concerns are the natural outgrowth of our renewed understanding of our ancient roots and of Jesus' own ministry as primarily one of reconciling the whole world.

Of course, this renewed understanding is not without its problems for "American" Catholics. Accustomed from our youth to think of church solely in terms of helping us "save our souls," and accustomed by our culture to praise rugged individualism and divisive competition, we are awkward and ill at ease when it comes to making the gestures of community and solidarity. If we are ever to become adept at it, we are going to have to be willing to place ourselves in situations and circumstances that allow us to give up our assertive and aggressive ways and learn the lessons of community, intimacy and solidarity. Only thus can we stop "living in sin."

The Christian Churches and Community

And, as has always been the case, when it comes to looking for help in coping with "sin" we are right-headed to look to the churches. All the more so once we see "sin" as the ultimate source of human fragmentation, and "salvation" as the struggle and attainment of reconciling wholeness. It is primarily from the churches that a voice has been raised against the isolation, the destructive competition, the irresponsible seeking of personal pleasure, the greed and injustice, and nuclear insanity, all of which have become taken-for-granted aspects of American life at the close of the twentieth century.

The New Testament ideal of reconciliation presents the Christian churches with a special challenge, one that they are only now beginning to attempt to meet. While reconciliation is proclaimed and is to be practiced most expressly within the Christian community itself, *it cannot be restricted to the circle of Christians,* but is to occur in the widest possible context of "world" reconciliation. Christians must take this universal outreach of reconciliation seriously. In that regard, the divisions within Christendom are the deepest and most profound of scandals. How can the Christian churches be about their appointed task of a ministry of peace and reconciliation, when they are themselves divided?

The truth is that nothing, absolutely nothing, takes precedence over reconciliation. Even worship of God must take second place to that, as we read in Matthew 5:23. Indeed, reconciliation with one's brothers and sisters is an essential precondition of true worship. Reconciliation is the topmost priority for Christians, so much so that readiness for reconciliation is the touchstone that determines whether a life, a movement, a program, a party, a community, a church are really "Christian" or not.

All sectarianism notwithstanding, the Christian churches are to show themselves to be "church" by moving across all the sociological, cultural, and religious boundaries that divide humankind. In a world torn by nationalism and religious sectarianism and division, it is the obligation of the Christian churches to incarnate and witness the unifying and reconciling power of Jesus. In the past, the Christian churches have too often been established along racial, cultural, national, or class lines. But in our time, they are finally beginning to join together in the common awareness of of their primary mission, reconciliation.

But as the churches recognize and act out of their common vocation and ministry, they are finding that the ministry of reconciliation requires them to become more involved in the social and political problems of our age. This is not only not foreign to the gospel messge, but is fidelity to its deepest essence. In our day, it is finally beginning to dawn on the churches that *sectarianism in any form is the primary heresy.* This deep awareness of our age, can only deepen and spread.

All this comes as no surprise to those of us who have been blessed with an experience of real "community" in our own lives. As we have already seen, salvation is an ongoing process, but for Christians and Jews it has also always been a place. As the great Jewish philosopher Martin Buber has said, "We expect a theophany of which we know nothing but the place. And the place? The place is called *community.*" For Jews and Christians a theophany, a meeting and encounter with the living God, always occurs incarnately, in the concrete places of this life. That's our heritage, our common faith. At times burdensome, at times frustrating, even boring at times, what keeps us at this task of forming "community," no matter what? The "theophanies," of course! Those rare and privileged moments when without warning Love (God) breaks through and makes its presence felt, revealing as it does the real meaning of salvation/reconciliation, and calling each one of us out of our own individual concerns, out beyond even our own small communities to a world that awaits "salvation."

Community: End or Means?

We read in Genesis (2:18): "It is not good for a human to be alone..." but the truth of the matter is that humans have never been alone. Nor does the Genesis account want to suggest that we ever were. It rather attempts to raise to fuller consciousness a truth that life revealed to humankind right from the start, namely that the coming together of people is something precious. What better way to help keep us mindful of this than for us to have put in the mouth of Yahweh the truism: "It is not good for a human to be alone"?

One reason ancient peoples recognized that it was not good to be alone was that a person could not survive in the harsh environment this way. It was only by coming together that life could be sustained, new life begun, and the quality of life improved. Because so many of the good things of life only become available to one because of cooperation with others of humankind, the coming together of human beings came to be seen as a means to an end. So it was that in the fourth century B.C.E. Aristotle could say with confidence: "Man is by nature a social animal and every community is established with a view to achieving something considered to be good."[13]

Aristotle was merely expressing a truth well established in human experience; no one would think of denying it. Nor did the early Christians deny it. Following the Lord's command to teach all nations (Matthew 28:19), the disciples went about setting up "faith communities" wherever they could. And the reason for those "faith communities," the good they sought to gain for their members was, of course, salvation (Mark 16:17). One entered a Christian community *in order to be saved,* and to associate and fraternize with others who were also saved. Quite clearly, then, the early Christians continued to view community in the accepted way—as a means to some other end.

For purposes of this discussion, let's agree to call all such groups or groupings formed for the purpose of acquiring or achieving some identifiable good *unions of convenience.* To qualify as a union of convenience all that is required is that human persons come together for some specific purpose other than their coming together. But that seems to include every sort of group. One is hard pressed to think of even one human group that does not fulfill this definition. All government agencies, businesses, political parties, fraternal organizations, parliaments, legislative and judicial bodies, all religious congregations, in fact every human grouping seems to be a union of convenience. Even those founded on or for love, *i.e.*, family, church, seem to be included. No wonder it has become a taken for granted assumption that community is *always* a way or means of getting something else.

Now while much of modern sociology seems to invite us to take "community" as a synonym for "union of convenience," I'd like to suggest that our experience invites us and in fact requires us to say otherwise.

For example, people gather for auditions in a local neighborhood theater group. Those chosen begin the process of learning lines, making scenery, sewing costumes, creating proper lighting and make-up, and the myriad tasks necessary to stage a successful play. After weeks of rehearsal and work, the play is presented, has a short run of about a week, and then suddenly it is all over. Those involved feel lost, they miss the rehearsals, they miss the hard work, there is an emptiness about them. The group gathers again to celebrate its successful venture but somehow there is more behind it all. The truth is they miss one another. They had become "bonded to one another" in a special way in virtue of their having been joined in a common project. They don't want it to end. They gather just to be together. It is at this point that what started out as a "union of convenience" has become a "potential community." And it is not unusual to find that people in such circumstances speak about their final cast-party as if it were a religious event, a kind of liturgy, which, of course, it certainly can be.

That example, and countless others from everyday experience, teaches us that some very wonderful and mysterious things can happen whenever human beings gather to combine their efforts in common work toward a common goal. It is true that in the dynamics of interpersonal relationships we often let our egos get in the way and develop harsh rivalries, deep dislikes and hatreds, cruel and insensitive competitions, as well as burning envies. But in such situations it is also possible for us to come to know and respect the other, to be supported by another's kindness and to offer similar support in return, to discover friendship, camaraderie, and even love. And when in the midst of our "unions of convenience" we do discover these things, then the good to be achieved by the common work, and even the common work itself becomes secondary. It is being together in solidarity that we prize.

It is at such moments that a union of convenience heralds the potential for community that always lies hidden within it. For such groupings can always become the occasion that invites us to move beyond seeing our relationships with others as means to some end of self-interest, and at that point the group becomes more than a union of convenience and can be called a potential community. That is, a nascent community about to be born, if only we don't become frightened and abort it.

What characterizes a potential community is that its members are on the verge of discovering one of life's most important truths, *i.e.*, that *community is really an end in itself.* Any common task or challenge has the power to precipitate this insight and open us up to this revelation. Nor is it even necessary that we be successful in accomplishing the task or meeting the challenge. Even in failure the beginnings of community can be forged.

Clearly, then, it is dangerous for women and men to come together for any purpose whatever, for it is always possible that in so doing they will discover life's secret: *Community and human solidarity are what human life is really all about.* Often we are not quite ready to hear this. We're not ready to open ourselves up to others quite *that* much.

For most of us, the revelation that community is an end in itself and not a means to anything else, that community is the goal of human life, comes only after a rather long and painful process of growth and development. We start by grouping with our fellow humans for the sake of convenience—to achieve some identifiable goal. Then we discover in those relationships of convenience the real truth about human life. Finally, we take the risk-filled step of trying to live out the truth our experience has revealed to us.

Fortunately for us, because life is shot through with God's presence, it is filled with manifold opportunities for us to learn the lesson of presence. Given the ambiguity of human nature we may have failed to respond as we know we should and must. No matter. There is always another opportunity right around the corner. An opportunity for us to finally live the secret of life we have come to know: it is not good for us to be alone.

Searching for Community

In these hard, dehumanizing times, there is a hunger abroad in the land, a hunger for the "human connection," "intimacy," and "a feeling of human solidarity." It is a hunger which even the American Dream cannot eradicate or assuage. People are gathering, clustering, huddling together as if to protect themselves from the elements, the withering winds of our technological, secular culture. This alienation, so characteristic of the United States, is largely invisible because it is the systematic strangulation and starvation of the human spirit. In growing throngs Americans run hither and yon in search of a saving place. And everywhere one hears the cry: "Where can we find it? How does one go about forming community?" It is a burning question for people. And of course everyone, including myself, has her or his favorite answer. But before going into this, it might be helpful to demythologize the enterprise by identifying some of the erroneous myths that surround it.

Myths About Community

In a marvelous little book entitled *The Promise of Paradox,* Parker Palmer lists three of the prevailing myths that govern our thinking about "community." I would like to reflect a bit on each of them here.

Myth 1 "...Community is an important creature comfort that can be added to the other creature comforts that grace our lives." What this comes down to is that "community" is sought as a means to an end, like any other consumer good. It is seen as something which enhances life and makes us more "advantaged" than those without it. Of course, as is the case these days in a culture governed by the law of supply and demand, it is dear and costly. So we find people "shopping" for all sorts of things that promise community, eager and willing to pay for the experience, to go into this kind of therapy or that, to buy this book or that, to enroll in this program or that—the litany is virtually endless. The truth, of course, is that *community is not for sale,* which is extremely bad news in a consumer culture like ours.

Myth 2 "...Community is a kind of utopia, and...we shall forge supportive relationships which will result in our all being brothers and sisters again." But experience shows that there is always pain in community, witness the exquisite pain which we have all experienced from time to time in the bosom of our own families. There is pain in not being able to have one's own way, there is pain in the clash of egos, and there is pain in the realization that I and my views are not the ultimate measure of reality. The truth is *there is no authentic community without pain.*

Myth 3 "...In keeping with our utopian dream (see Myth 2), we think we have community when we establish deep and intimate associations with people who are just like ourselves, people who in almost every respect are clones of our own interests and desires." While it is true that solidarity is an essential characteristic of community, it certainly is not the case that community requires homogeneity. In fact, experience teaches us that it is just the opposite. *Authentic community is never homogeneous or sectarian.*

Why all the fuss? What is Palmer getting at? For one thing, how one thinks of community makes a big difference in the way one goes about forming, achieving, and building it. Or to put the matter the other way around, if one thinks community can be bought; that it can be achieved without effort, tears, or pain; that it means bonding with people who are similiar in background, aspirations, and tastes; then it is doubtful one will ever be successful. One will be looking for community in the wrong places, for the wrong reasons, and in the wrong way.

Building Community

While it is true that community is really an end in itself and not a means to something else, especially not our personal happiness, it is wrong-headed to think that the way to achieve it is to make "forming community" the direct objective of one's actions. Strange as it may seem, it doesn't work that way. If you want to form community you must aim at something else, and community will come as a by-product. Palmer puts it well:

> Community is another one of those strange things which eludes us if we aim directly at it. Instead, community comes as a by-product of commitment and struggle. *It comes when we step forward to right some wrong, to heal some hurt, to give some service. Then we discover each other as allies in resisting the diminishments of life.* It

> is no accident that the most impressive sense of community is found among people in the midst of such joyful travail: among blacks, among women, among all who have said no to tyranny with the yes of their lives.[14]

Now we can see what Palmer was driving at with all his talk of avoiding the prevailing myths about community. At the root of it all is the common misunderstanding that "community" can be sought directly. It is the by-product of commitment and struggle. The question "Where can I find community?" is precisely the wrong question. The right question is: "What are the prevailing diminishments in life that are currently crushing me, and my sisters and brothers?" The best strategy for forming community is to take up arms against those sources of diminishment, alienation, and division. In so doing, community will inevitably happen. Like all the truly important things in human life, "community" is something that happens to us on the way as we seek something else. Paradoxically, to find the saving place I seek for myself, I must gather with my sisters and brothers to right some wrong, heal some pain, give some service, or resist the diminishments of human life wherever they occur. Only then will community happen. It will happen as a "gift" from the God who is present in our lives, and who in the end is the one who enables us to be "present" to one another. The community we seek will not come simply because we want it. It will come only as we are willing to shoulder one another's burdens, pick up one another's crosses, and in the process find ourselves no longer isolated individuals but part of a people. This is the sure and proven way.

Community as Novitiate for Salvation/Reconciliation

As sought after as community is, it is all too often sought after as a source of individual fulfillment to be achieved without the struggle and pain of changing and transforming one's inner self. As if I could reap the benefits of community without transforming my modes of being present to the world. This is totally unrealistic. Community is as demanding as boot-camp, or the noviceship, and for exactly the same reasons. It requires profound changes within the individual, changes which alter one's view of reality, and one's ultimate aspirations. This is never child's play. It requires a great degree of maturity, and is particularly difficult for Americans like us, who were raised to be self-reliant and beholden to no one.

Community is the place where we learn the basic lessons of our humanity, how to be human, how to become a beneficent and life-giving presence, how to love and to reconcile, and most of all how to go about unlearning the isolating individualistic mores of our American heritage. Talking community is easy, living it is the greatest challenge of our lives.

This is such a challenge because we are very ambivalent about it. We both desire it and flee from it. We see it as the fulfillment of ourselves, as well as fetters that give others a claim on us. Torn between those opposing views, we find it difficult, if not impossible, to give ourselves totally to community. We are afraid that this would be giving ourselves away. Given our vacillating attitude, no wonder we never seem to find a lasting community, and the history of our time is one of ever widening fragmentation and disintegration.

To break out of the ambiguity, we must learn or relearn the moves and gestures of bondedness, we must from experience still our fears that we shall be swallowed up by the group and lose our identity, we must begin to feel empowered and not depleted by community. The way to go about this is to somehow translate our private problems and aspirations into communal ones. And the place to begin to work on those things is within an identifiable community of some sort. It is in community that I learn that I cannot live in isolation, that my life is intertwined with others, and that I am accountable for my actions to someone beyond myself. It is in community that I learn that power and domination are not really successful strategies of human behavior in the long run. It is from the community that I find the support to risk being a Kingdom person.

All this can be learned from community, and still I resist. What is it that keeps me from being open enough to learn the lessons of community ? For most of us, it is the unwillingness to appear flawed and broken in the eyes of others. We are "present" only in ways that allow no one into our real self, and we remain content to present to the world only a public persona, a mask that hides the contradictions and brokenness we experience at our centers. We think we're the only ones experiencing such things. But as we learn to share our brokenness, and give up the desire to appear flawless, we find that others are empowered by our sharing to do the same, and suddenly there is a power unleashed out of brokenness and weakness of which there is no like in all the world. The power of community is, paradoxically, absolutely dependent on the sharing of weakness. *There is no other way.* This explains the tremendous salvific power of Alcoholics Anonymous, of various support groups, and of base communities in our time. So long as we allow others no way into our brokenness, there can be no saving place for the individual, there can be no reconciliation for the world, there can be no life together.

Community seems to be beyond our reach, an impossible dream, egotism is just too strong and individualism too widespread. Unions of convenience seem to be all that humankind can manage these days. Such a dark view may well arise in many all around us, but, as believers, we cannot succumb to such a bleak assessment of the human condition. Have we forgotten the malaise and deep hunger that spread like famine across the earth? Have we forgotten, despite all the obstacles, that we humans have been made to live life together? Have we forgotten that we are not alone and that God is incarnated in human life precisely to keep it from fragmentation and disintegration, and that community among human beings is the result of that presence? And finally, have we forgotten the many women and men in our lives whose presence to and among us has witnessed to not only the possibility of community, but to its absolute inevitability? To have forgotten *all* of that is what it means to have lost the faith.

In this secular culture of ours, this is all too easy to do. For in the end, community is a spiritual or religious reality, not merely a social one. *Our culture would agree, and have no part of it.* Because it takes "spiritual" in a non-incarnational sense, it leaves the work of community up to the churches, as we have seen. That's their job, just so long as they don't attempt to change the status quo. But community is always subversive of the secular order, because the secular order, precisely as secular, is prevented from factoring incarnation into the social equation. It cannot see, or does not believe that community is not an otherworldly phenomenon, but the overflow of God's loving presence into *this* world, aimed at transforming, that is, saving, it.

Those who do see and believe this, are on a collision course with today's culture, because they are moved to share the love they have discovered in community with the disadvantaged, the exploited, the poor and the wounded, the number of whom is growing daily. The confrontation of two opposing forces and value systems creates tension within the hearts of those who want to be good citizens, and want also to walk with God. It is to the consideration of this tension that we turn next.

CHAPTER SIX

THE "AMERICAN" ETHOS

To "Americanize" immigrants is not an easy thing to do, because they come to the United States having been formed and fashioned by the ethos of their countries of origin. If they are to succeed in the America of today, they must acquire certain attitudes and skills; only then will they be accepted as truly "American." Many of us who were born and raised here acquired these skills easily, so we are blissfully unaware of what a truly wrenching experience it can be for one formed otherwise. Moving to any new culture is always difficult, but becoming "American" is peculiarly difficult because it demands profound changes in one's inner space.

Americanization means learning to live by a new set of myths or stories, it means accepting the "American way" of thinking and acting, the values and mores that format one's inner space so that one fits into the mainstream of American life. In *theory*, it means accepting the ideals of liberty and justice for all as put forth by the founders of the Republic in the Declaration of Independence and the Constitution. In *practice*, what it really comes down to is adopting the current American interpretation of liberty, and the consumption-based lifestyles to which it gives rise. This contemporary interpretation of liberty and freedom is so far removed from our origins that many are beginning to question whether it is realistic to think the nation can survive on its present course.

Elements of the "American" Character: A Look in the Mirror

In 1979 a team of social researchers led by Robert Bellah began a study of the American middle class, and after five years of study produced their results in a book entitled *Habits of the Heart*.[15] It immediately became a national best seller, about which *Newsweek* said: "A brilliant analysis...easily the richest and most readable study of American society since the 50's...." It is all of that and more. The researchers themselves thought of their work as the continuation of the study of the American character done in the 1830s by the French social philosopher Alexis de Tocqueville entitled *Democracy In America*.[16] Tocqueville's account of the mores of American society, which he at times called "habits of the heart" (the phrase chosen by Bellah and company as the title for their book), was filled with much admiration for America, but also with insightful warnings about those elements in its national character that, if left unchecked, had the potential to undermine the noble experiment of freedom.

The Bellah book, then, is a contemporary assessment of the state of the American character in the 1980s and an appraisal of the validity of Tocqueville's warnings as well as a prescription for changes in character (our inner space) if "freedom" is to survive in America.

Individualism As Bellah and his team did their research, they began to wonder whether "equality" really was the basic foundation for American life as is so often portrayed. Their studies indicated to them that the real constant throughout our history has been "individualism." Bellah writes:

> Individualism lies at the very core of American culture. We believe in the dignity, indeed the sacredness, of the individual. Anything that would violate our right to think for ourselves, judge for ourselves, make our own decisions, live our lives as we see fit, is not only morally wrong, it is sacrilegious. Our highest and noblest aspirations, not only for ourselves, but for those we care about, for our society and for the world, are closely linked to our individualism. (p. 142).

But he wonders whether whether individualism may not have gotten out of hand in our times, become cancerous, and threatening to the very freedom of the nation.

> It seems to us that it is individualism, and not equality, that has marched inexorably through our history. We are concerned that this individualism may have grown cancerous—that it may be destroying those social integuments that moderate its more destructive potentialities, that it may be threatening the survival of freedom itself. We want to know what individualism in America looks and feels like, and how the world appears in its light (p. vii).

One is tempted to say that if they want to know what individualism looks like in our day, ask any parent, any teacher, any employer, indeed anyone in a position of authority who must work with other people. They can tell you first-hand; they deal with it every day.

In the 1830s, Tocqueville gave a chilling definition of individualism, but it sounds very much like a description of life today in the United States.

> Individualism is a word recently coined to express a new idea. Our fathers only knew about egoism. Individualism is a calm and considered feeling which disposes each citizen to isolate himself from the mass of his fel-

> lows and withdraw into the circle of family and friends; with this little society formed to his taste, he gladly leaves the greater society to look after itself. There are more and more people who though neither rich nor powerful enough to have much hold over others have gained or kept enough wealth and enough understanding to look after their own needs. Such folk owe no man anything and hardly expect anything from anybody. They form the habit of thinking of themselves in isolation and imagine that their whole destiny is in their hands. Such people come to "forget their ancestors," but also their descendants, as well as isolating themselves from their contemporaries. Each man is forever thrown back on himself alone, and there is danger that he may be shut up in the solitude of his own heart. (pp. 506-508)

Undoubtedly for Tocqueville, individualism is an admirable trait in contrast to egoism because it has the note of self-reliance about it. But he seems to raise the possibility that, unlike genuine virtue, one can have too much individualism. Too much of it leads to a certain convenient forgetfulness of one's ancestors, of one's contemporaries, and of the communal enterprise in which we are all involved. When this happens, each one is shut up in selfish, prideful isolation, which destroys the very bonds that hold the republic together. For Tocqueville this constitutes the greatest threat to hard-won American freedom.

Bellah goes on to raise the question as to whether what Tocqueville foresaw is not exactly what characterizes American society today. It is a purely rhetorical question for him because he obviously thinks it does. Bellah distinguishes two main types of a rampant "social cancer" of our time.

The first and most virulent form of "disease" rests on the assumption that the only reason individuals form societies at all is to further their own self-interests. Society is the result of a sort of contract between individuals acting solely for their own gains, especially in terms of money, power, and social status. This is the most "rugged" of individualisms, and the most fanatical practitioners of it argue that the social good of all can emerge only in a society where each person single-mindedly and passionately pursues self-interest. No need, then, to have anyone charged and responsible for looking after the common interests of all; government's main task is to create the proper conditions for fair and open competition where the strongest prevail. This is called *utilitarian individualism.*

This form of individualism, so prevalent in nineteenth century America, is so insensitive, mean-minded, and brutish, that it was bound to be challenged in the name of our humanity. So it was. While the majority of males reveled in the utilitarian contest, many women, poets, and the clergy raised their voices against the dehumanizing effects of such a life. (At the same time in Europe the young Marx was raising the same issue.) What do you profit if you gain the whole world and never give expression to your true self? This became the question. The quest for a truer freedom than money could buy, the freedom of being your own person, of giving expression to your own inner self emerged.

To this end, one would have to break free of all the bogus controls imposed on the individual by business, family, and society. The goal was to insure that you truly live *your* life, the life crying to emerge from deep within. Money, power, and social status are not the main constituents of satisfying the demands of that inner life. So it was that there arose an alternative to utilitarian individualism, an alternative that was more sensitive, more humane, but no less individualistic. Because this form of individualism stresses the importance of personal experience and the need to express one's inner feelings for a successful life, Bellah calls it *expressive individualism.*

These two types of individualism pretty much determine the current American definition of and attitude toward success. To be successful and to be viewed so by their peers, Americans must triumph in the highly competitive world of the work place, *and* at the same time be uninhibited enough to give full expression to their emotions and authentic selves in their home and personal lives. What creates the tension so characteristic of our culture is that the skills and habits of heart that bring success in one of these areas are often in direct variance with those that do so in the other. Be that as it may, whether at work, or home, or play, we Americans make a prodigious effort to succeed.

Self-Reliance However we Americans define success, an essential element in our definition is that we have achieved it on our own. We do not and cannot view ourselves as successful unless we can show that our advancement in the work place and our fulfillment and satisfaction in our personal lives are due to our own efforts. The American self-image depends on this.

Like individualism, the drive to self-reliance is an admirable trait—within limits. Beyond these limits, it too becomes cancerous, eating away at the very muscle and sinew of society. In the past the drive to be self-reliant was seen as something of a communal enterprise since it was in the interests of the group to have its members be able to stand on their own feet, all the better to contribute. In our day, the drive for self-reliance has come to mean the need to be self-sufficient, to be totally independent of and totally unencumbered by others. We speak less and less about a shared liberty, and more and more about personal freedom. Thus freedom has come to mean some sort of total and complete autonomy.

In the name of freedom, America's young people are being raised on the ideal of unencumbered self-reliance. They rush to "leave home," to "leave church," to jettison the values of not only their parents and church but of their nation as well. So imbued are they with the goal of doing it on their own, that they view any contribution from outside their autonomous selves as unwelcome and an unjustified interference. They feel the pressure "to make something of themselves," and understand that to mean "to make themselves." And so they try. Adults often seem envious of the young by lamenting that things were not so free when they were growing up. They reason that freedom "American style" should not be wasted on the young. So they try, too. The results are as destructive as they were predictable, and constitute, for Tocqueville and Bellah, a greater threat to liberty than any foreign power ever could.

Reaping the Fruits of Our National Character

Individualism and self-reliance are attitudes of mind that affect the inner space of Americans so that they view the world in a peculiarly "American way." This way of viewing our world manifests itself most clearly, however, in our actions, and in the way we are "present" to one another and to our world. Bellah and his team spend much of their book analysing the many consequences of our current mind-set, but for purposes of contrasting the American and Catholic experiences, I want to share what they say about only four of them: *Work, Therapy, Life-style,* and *Love.*

Work: "American Style" There is so much talk about the drudgery of work, of how glorious it would be to win the lottery, or retire and be freed from the burden of work, that it is very easy to overlook or misunderstand the importance of work in the American scheme of things. The fact is, work seems tailor-made to bring the two forms of American individualism together. Not that the work most people do is an expression of their deepest most authentic selves. Not at all. Only a small minority find themselves that blessed. But the devastation to the economics of the family and to the self-esteem of bread-winners wrought by unemployment clearly shows how essential work is for both the economic and personal success of the individual. Work is the cornerstone of both self-reliance and self-esteem. One's work defines one's self in some profound and essential way. We have not only been made in the image of God, we have been made in the image of God *the Creator.* What we do and how and why we do it affect who we are; they make us certain kinds of people.

Many lament today that the old "work ethic" has disappeared. Without denying that, Bellah thinks that the more serious problem is the meaning of work and the way it bonds, or fails to bond, individuals to one another (p. 56). Thinking along these lines, he distinguishes three different ways of looking at work, each depending on how the worker views its meaning (p. 66).

For some work is just a *job.* It is a way of making money, of getting the wherewithal simply to live and survive, or to live well by improving one's standard of living. Since economic well-being is an integral part of what Americans take as success, one needs a "job" to get all the things that money can buy. Such a stance vis-a-vis one's work yields a self determined in large measure by utilitarian individualism.

For others work is not only a job, it is also a *career.* In this situation one's job not only affords one a living, even a good one, it also enhances one's self-image. Career people are more apt to take pride in what they do, to see their work as a part of their own personal journey. As "career," one's work marks one's personal achievement, traces one's advancement from beginner apprentice to experienced master or professional. A "career" yields a richer kind of self for the worker. It gives one social standing, prestige, and enhances one's importance and self-worth. Work as "career" links one's job and way of earning a living more closely to the development of the self, and is therefore an important element in expressive individualism.

But there is an ideal which takes work beyond the realm of individualism altogether. It occurs when one no longer sees what one does merely as a way to make a living, nor even as a path to personal fulfillment in terms of career goals, but as one's way of making a contribution to the common life of the community, as one's *calling*. It is precisely as "calling" that work has the capacity to link one to a whole in which what one does transcends both utilitarian and expressive self-interest and is a contribution to the good of all.

If this sounds idealistic, it is probably because individualism has become so widespread and virulent that any thought of working for other than personal goals strikes us as unrealistic. But in a world where the self is the only goal how can we expect anything more than inferior products and degrading service? If working means to fit something into its proper place in a greater whole, the absence of a sense of "calling" deprives our work of any real meaning. When one's work lacks this kind of meaning, people seek it in other areas, and as we might expect they often seek for meaning in some form of expressive individualism, pursuing it in their private lives with friends, family and those who share their lifestyle. The meaninglessness and triviality of so much of the work people are asked to do has forced them to seek the meaning of their lives in private isolation, away from the work place and the community. This has therefore contributed mightily to the spread of our individualistic cancer.

Work, which has the potential for bonding people together in a common enterprise beyond self-interest, has been reduced, in the minds of growing numbers of people, especially the young who have never known another time than this, to an unwelcome burden. Having a job may be important to one's self-interest and self-image, but actually working on that job is quite another thing. Once one comes to see meaning and fulfillment to be strictly private matters, it is difficult to put one's heart into work. One dreams of the weekend, the next coffee break, the next cruise, the next ski trip, the next vacation; in short, one looks for ways of *getting out of work.* The traditional American "work ethic" has fallen on hard times.

If this is so, what beyond mere survival keeps Americans working? Money, status, and success. And the competition for those things is fierce. So fierce and utilitarian that again we find the impetus of American life away from the crowd toward the more peaceful private life, where one can find some surcease from the struggle and nurture one's authentic inner self. Indeed, the unrelenting competition is only tolerable so long as one has a place, a "saving" place, to let down one's defenses and relate to others in a non-competitive way. By contrast to the world of competitive and frantic work, the more quiet private world of personal expression becomes ever more attractive. But the question then becomes, is one, who is present in a competitive way in the utilitarian world of work all day, really able to be present in relational and expressive ways at home and at play? Certainly it becomes more and more difficult to do so. The tension between the ways of the world of work and the ways of the world of personal relationships is strongly felt as people try to integrate them and make sense of their lives. Each year the inability to integrate the utilitarian and expressive dimensions of American life drives more and more of us to seek the help of counselors and therapists.

Therapy: The American Way of Presence Americans these days seek therapeutic help on so broad a scale and in such burgeoning numbers, that therapy is no longer a minority experience, but has become an integral part of our very way of life. So much so, that Bellah actually suggests that the therapeutic relationship has become a type or model for Americans of how one is to live one's life. The American way of "presence," if you will.

The very word "therapy" suggests that all is not well with us, that something about the present situation needs to be changed, needs to be cured. Something about life in America these days is not as it should be. Bellah suggests that that something is the lack of fit between the developing and emerging self and the public expressions of that self allowed by our culture (p. 47). The "cure" people seek from therapists is some way to empower the individual self to be able to cope with the often conflicting demands of work and intimacy. Somehow, they feel impotent in the face of the overwhelming social pressures inherent in our way of life.

In the past, people sought such help from religion, or from the community, but in our secularized, individualistic culture those sources of caring help have lost their attractiveness and legitimacy. The fear is that the individual will somehow fare badly in these contexts, will lose control and become "encumbered." The greatest virtue of therapy is that the therapist is one's very own advocate, someone whose sole aim is to work for my personal interests, someone who will listen to my story, however skewered or sordid, without being judgmental. The therapist leaves me in control. No threat to my freedom, no threat to my self-reliance. Quite the contrary, the therapist works to make me more free and more self-reliant amid the insanities of my everyday life. No wonder therapists are so sought after. As the stigma of being in therapy lessens, those who can afford it will avail themselves of such marvelous therapeutic experiences.

It is no accident that the rise of the importance of therapy coincides with the rise of individualism. There is something very special and enigmatic, yet so typically "American," about the therapeutic relationship. Therapy is a relationship that combines a certain professional objectivity and restraint with the deepest kind of intimacy and sharing. This latter characteristic, as an exercise in presence, has the potential to make it even sacred. The restraint follows upon the fact that it is a relationship between a patient (better called a "client") and a professional therapist. The client seeks something for himself or herself from the professional expertise of the therapist, and is willing and able to pay for those services. A contractual (business) agreement is entered into, spelling out the terms of the relationship and calling for an exchange of the client's money for the therapist's time. Success, because it cannot be guaranteed, is generally not one of the terms of the contract; it is a simple exchange of money and time. So the therapeutic relationship is a very strange mixture of business and intimacy, joining the utilitarian and expressive dimensions of life into some sort of meaningful whole.

Such a description, however, hardly does the therapeutic

relationship justice. Its genius is to afford, from that very strange mixture of business and caring, a context where it is safe for people to examine and share the deeper elements of their lives. Therapy thus becomes a saving place for the client. That is no small matter these days and, as we have seen, is never to be underestimated.

Perhaps the most remarkable thing about therapy is the rather modest ways and means it uses to achieve its goal. Often it is the therapist/client relationship itself which is the major factor in whatever success is achieved. That relationship forces the client to examine his or her life, to attempt to see the meaning of the scattered fragments and to strive to communicate feelings, aspirations, and desires. The client talks. The therapist listens, truly listens, as the client's story unfolds. It is a real "gift" to have someone truly listen to you. It loosens your tongue, frees you from inhibitions, and suddenly you are saying and telling things to your therapist that you've never told anyone before. Sometimes things you never realized before become suddenly clear in the context of therapy. And you do it in the confidence that you need not be afraid, that it is safe to share, that nothing you say will be used against you by your therapist. By contrast to the utilitarian world where you must succeed and compete, by contrast to your personal life where the pressure is to make accommodation for others and to meet their ever increasing expectations of you, here in this "saving" therapeutic place you have a new life-giving experience. Perhaps for the first time in your life, you feel total acceptance and experience the miracle of what that does for you. You are accepted just the way you are, with all your strengths and all your brokenness. And also, perhaps for the first time, you feel a power and a freedom emerge from deep within you, a power and freedom you had forgotten you possessed or never knew you had.

Is it any wonder, then, that therapy has become an integral part of American life? It is the closest thing that many in our country have to a "religious" experience. The patient, non-assertive, non-demanding, accepting posture of the therapist is undoubtedly a reflection of what believers would call the absolute and unconditional love of God for humankind. And like that divine love which it reflects, it cannot help but be "healing," *i.e.*, therapeutic.

There in the protected and somewhat artificial atmosphere of the therapeutic relationship you begin to see who you really are, and what you really want. The decision must be made to find appropriate ways of giving expression to your true self, and of achieving what it is you really want within the context of the "givens" in your work and personal life. You are going to have to stop always deferring to others, to become independent of their standards and values, and start living by your own. People are going to have to take you and your needs more into account. But they can only do that if you frankly communicate to them what those needs are and do not silently suppose that because they live and work with you they should "just know." Changes may have to be made. Even profound and painful ones.

Clearly, though therapy attempts to mediate the demands of utilitarian and expressive individualism on the client, in the end it comes down heavily on the side of individual expression. Indeed, it puts the individual at the center of things, and sees work and personal relationships as so many "enhancements" of the individual. That way of viewing things is what Bellah calls the *therapeutic attitude*. It has become our predominant American mind-set.

Lifestyle vs. Community In one of the more insightful applications of this therapeutic attitude, Bellah, with keen discernment, distinguishes *communities* from what he labels *lifestyle enclaves* (p. 72). He thinks that the word "community" is bandied about much too loosely. It is applied to groupings that are not in the slightest communal. He suggests that it might be better to use another term for those associations that flourish in our society where members remain totally unencumbered. They do not exhibit the features of a true community, but they are the prevailing social groupings in our individualistic and therapeutic culture. He calls them *lifestyle enclaves*.

Since words do not arise for no reason, it is interesting to note how prevalent the word "lifestyle" has become in our language in the past 20 years. The word came into use precisely because we had need of it to name the social phenomenon of how people cluster with one another when the prevailing myth is individualism, and the prevailing attitude therapeutic. People who cluster with others so as to enhance the self are said to share a given lifestyle. When we speak of a person's lifestyle we usually are not talking about that person in terms of job or work, but primarily in terms of how one uses leisure time, where one shops, what one buys, in what circles one moves in living one's life away from the work place. In short, lifestyle has to do primarily with habits of consumption and leisure.

Whereas community is open and inclusive, people are explicitly contrasted into different groupings according to lifestyle. I am always divided from those who do not share my lifestyle. Indeed, should I succeed in making a great deal of money, a good portion of it will undoubtedly be spent to guarantee that such divisions be respected and enforced. This characteristic of dividing people caused Bellah to say that a "lifestyle community" is really a misnomer. Lifestyle by nature is segmental and divisive, and so he preferred to call such groupings *enclaves*, indeed "lifestyle enclaves."

It is precisely their segmental nature that makes lifestyle enclaves so perfectly suited to today's therapeutically sensitized, self-reliant individuals. When one thinks of one's bridge buddies, one's fishing pals, one's sewing circle, the gang one goes to the game with, it is clear that participation in such groups relies entirely on the individual's voluntary participation. One chooses to participate, and one chooses to participate only within very narrow boundaries. One shares with enclave members only those "segments" of one's personality that one chooses to share and that are appropriate, given the nature of the group. I can plug into and pull out of a lifestyle enclave at will. I call the shots. I remain in control. I am never obliged to share my "whole" self. Membership in such a group leaves me absolutely unencumbered. I remain free to live my own life in my own way. How utterly "American"!

This is not to suggest that there is anything wrong with lifestyle enclaves; they are important and necessary elements of everyday life. Were it not for them, the loneliness brought on by our passion for unencumbered freedom would be unbearable. Lifestyle enclaves give us a sense of connectedness, of belonging, of making a difference. Besides, every lifestyle enclave always has the potential for becoming community, and a place where I can share my whole self and am open to such sharing from the others. To denigrate lifestyle enclaves is not only misguided, it is cruel. People need to be connected, and good things happen whenever and wherever people gather. Lifestyle enclaves may not be communities in the fullest sense, but at present they may be all that Americans imbued with individualism and the therapeutic attitude are capable of.

Love: "American Style" Individualism and the enclave mentality have also, in our day, not unexpectedly redefined love relationships, marriage, and family. Once the epitome of community, American marriages today look more and more like lifestyle enclaves, in which, when the liaison no longer serves the individual interests of one of the parties, the marriage is summarily terminated. Personal love relationships and marriage are viewed in strictly individualistic terms as enhancements of the individual, and when the relationship ceases to be personally enhancing, it is discarded in the name of freedom and authenticity. The divorce rate has soared as a consequence.

In our day, marriage has become separated from the communal and social context of family, if for no other reason than that, for growing numbers of Americans, marriage no longer implies having children at all. One's marriage is the private place and context of expressive individualism wherein one can escape the public conflict and strife. Should it fail to fulfill me and offer me such a haven, it is no longer seen as enhancing in my life, and the only honest and authentic thing to do is to end it. Of course, to see marriage as a relationship I am at liberty to plug into or pull out of at will reduces marriage to the status of a lifestyle enclave.

On the other hand, marriage partners are expected to adopt the therapeutic attitude toward one another. Each in turn listens sensitively to the other, striving for open and authentic communication, all the while assessing whether the relationship is mutually beneficial enough to warrant continuing in it. This fact caused Bellah to remark: "The present ideology of American individualism has difficulty justifying why men and women should be giving themselves to one another at all" (p. 111). Why indeed, if you are more enhancing to me as my lover than as my spouse? So it is that marriage as traditionally understood has fallen upon hard times in America.

And, as we might have expected, so too has the family. As familial relationships come also to be viewed primarily as enhancements of individual family members, the family in its turn is viewed as a lifestyle enclave. Whether family members, once adult, continue to relate to their parents or their sisters and brothers becomes a matter of choice, subject to individual negotiation and veto. The American family has in many ways become *optional.* Beset by extraordinary pressures from without, and plagued by divisive individualism from within, one of the present-day miracles of American life is the survival of the family at all.

Contemporary America: A Critique

As far back as the middle of the last century, Tocqueville identified the seeds of the present situation, and foresaw the consequences we are now experiencing. But he perhaps was more hopeful about our prospects back then than many of us are today. The reason was because in addition to naming the emergence of individualism and foretelling where it would lead, he also identified certain factors in our national life that would mitigate our individualism, thus preventing it from becoming a cancer. Unfortunately, he had no way of knowing then that our love affair with individualism would cause us to reject those very saving elements from our national life.

Tocqueville identified three things he felt could keep Americans from self-destructing on individualism: *Religion, Family,* and *Public Service.* Each called the individual forth to some real concern beyond the self. Each is based on a person's willingness to be encumbered for the sake of others. He thought that those things constituted a kind of "immune system" against the cancer of individualism. So long as those things remained strong and vital elements in American life, individualism would be properly counter-balanced and would remain a characteristic American virtue and not become an isolating and destructive vice.

One could truthfully say that since World War II there has been a constant erosion of our "immune system" against individualism. Where religion has not been totally rejected, it has been trivialized or subverted to the status of an individual enhancement. Public life and service are ridiculed as not worthy of our best minds and talents, and the public corruption that subverts public office to individual interests has become so widespread as to have totally destroyed the image of public service as "calling." Having held out the longest against the ravages of our cancer, the American family has in its turn finally begun to collapse all around us. With all the traditional safeguards down, there is little left to protect our young people (or ourselves for that matter) from the epidemic, the plague, of individualism.

Of course, believers and their institutions are not exempt from the effects of all this on their faith lives. American Christians are daily faced with the challenge of what in the current American ethos is compatible with the Good News of the gospels, and what isn't. American Catholics are especially challenged as Pope John Paul II calls into question the compatibility of many cherished American values with the traditional Catholic ethos. In his last visit to the United States, he effectively said "no" to every issue raised by the American bishops in behalf of the "American" church. Using American individualism as an excuse and reason for his intransigence on every issue raised, he effectively proclaimed that the Catholic church could never change just to suit the desires of its people. Especially not the desires of individualistic and therapeutically-minded Americans. If they don't like it, they will just have to leave.

Of course, two wrong stances don't make a right stance. So it is entirely possible to disagree both with the current American value system, and disagree as well with the absolutist and parochial views of the pope. In fact, this is the case with the majority of believing American Catholics.

There can be no doubt that the American ethos and lifestyle are deserving of criticism in the name of both humanity and faith. The pope is certainly right about that. And he is also quite correct, I want to add, when he says that the Catholic church cannot change just to please the people. There is only one reason for the church to change, and that is *because it has been wrong*. Being unable or unwilling to admit that, John Paul II has chosen to use our current cultural malaise as a kind of scapegoat for his own unwillingness to allow changes validated and confirmed by the presence of God in the experiences of people. The Catholic church *must* change, not indeed to please its people, but because it has been wrong on so many things and because it is called to be true not only to the divine revelation of the past but also to the divine revelation in its present membership. The Catholic church *will* change, because if it doesn't it will cease to be "church."

The American Experience as Revelatory

The current signs are, however, that it will not change gracefully. It will resist. It will censure, berate, and condemn many more of us American Catholics before it is through. But in the end, whatever revelation there is in the our experience will prevail, as it always has in the church.

While Americans may presently be overstating the significance of individualism and understating the importance of human bondedness and mutual encumbrance, their experience does not. That is to say, our spoken cultural values are contradicted by the widespread pain and inner dissatisfaction they bring. There is little joy in the land. We have become so joyless a people that we constantly party, drinking and drugging ourselves into unconsciousness so as not to have to bear it. There is an unnamed hunger in us for we know not exactly what. But there just has to be more to life than *this*. Though it may take awhile, since our cultural values are so ingrained in us as to have become second nature, we cannot indefinitely ignore the dissatisfaction of so much of American life. God is in that hunger, in that dissatisfaction, revealing to us the possibility of a better, more fulfilling way.

God is in the hunger to be rid of nuclear and chemical weapons, the hunger for peace. God is in the hunger for justice. God is in the hunger of women for full recognition of their humanity. God is in the hunger for a sex life that is incarnational and "makes love." God is in the hunger for work that is meaningful and significant. God is in the hunger for a liberty without addiction. God is in the hunger for intimacy and the human connection. God is in the hunger of people to have children. God is in the hunger of children for loving and responsible parents. God is present in all our hungers, revealing to us what it is that is truly good and will really satisfy. America may look like it has abandoned God, but God has never abandoned us.

Amid all these hungers, fundamentalist religions have experienced a marked resurgence. And while they may have a salutary effect in the short run, in the long run they give rise to additional sorts of dissatisfactions and to their own special set of hungers, a sure sign that fundamentalist conformity is no answer to an individualism that has gone too far.

While it may be true on the surface that the current American ethos and the Catholic church are incompatible and seem to be on a collision course, there may be a deeper, more basic American ethos that isn't. Instead of fostering and appealing to those deeper dimensions of the American experience, Rome seems to have opted to treat its American members as children, scolding and cajoling like an irate parent, threatening us with reprimands should we not accept and quietly revert to traditional "Catholic" ways. That approach seems to be based on two assumptions. The first is that only a return to a strict discipline of the past will cure our social cancer, and the second is that those traditional ways of the church of Rome are really "Catholic." Of course, both assumptions are wrong. And to that aspect of the issue of being American *and* Catholic we turn in Chapter Eight after the following brief, personal interlude.

CHAPTER SEVEN

A PERSONAL INTERLUDE

Before turning, in the concluding chapter—to a consideration of such questions as: What does it mean to be Catholic?, Is it really possible to be both American *and* Catholic? Why would any American *want* to be Catholic?—I would like to share a special experience and gift with the reader. I do so in the hope that it will both further clarify what has already been said about "presence," and serve as an apt introduction to the concluding reflections of what it means to be Catholic.

On a hot and humid day in the summer of 1986, I received a

letter from an East Coast publisher asking permission to reprint something I had written years before. To better dispose me to give the permission, the editor kindly enclosed a copy of a parable by Francis Sullivan for my edification. It was mysteriously entitled simply *A Parable,* thereby giving no further indication of its message. Years later, and to this day, I cherish that as a special day on which I was truly graced. I shall forever be in Sullivan's debt. His parable touched me deeply, and illumined a truth that had been aborning in my own brain. I never miss a chance to share it with others, in the hope of affording them a similar experience of grace. Without warning or explanation, let me simply present it for your consideration here.

A Parable, by Francis P. Sullivan

A Buddhist monk found a christian child abandoned on the road one day. She was wearing a wooden cross around her neck and a cotton T-shirt that draped around her tiny frame. "She's only five years old," the monk said. There were few christians in the area, he did not know where. But he met a traveling priest whom he stopped to give him the child. And the priest said, "I am about to die. I have just the strength to get myself home. She would be abandoned again after a few miles." And the priest stood there for the monk's response. The monk said, "I am not allowed to deal with women young or old. I will lose myself." "Then leave us here," the priest said. "No," said the monk, "it will be worse for me if I leave her with you. I will take her until I find someone. May you find peace in death." "And may you find peace in life," the priest responded, and he left that place.

"Take hold of my robe," said the monk, "and we will walk until we find someone for you." But he found no one to care for her, to teach the girl child. People thought he was a monk gone bad, that this was his own child he made-believe was a christian. He got less and less food in his begging for the two of them until her life was in the balance with his own. So he said, "I will become a christian for the time that she is growing, and I will care for her, and I will teach her, then let her go in her maturity and she will find her own way. I will then return to my own belief, and may I be forgiven." So he taught her about creation, and she said, "O, how good that is !" Then he taught her about destruction, and she said, "O how bad !" Then he taught her about the Christ who absorbed destruction in order to recreate the world, and she said, "O, how good he is !" Then he taught her about the judgment, and the paradise, and the place of punished souls, and she said, "O, how good and bad that is !" Then he taught her about herself, and she said, "O, how good and bad I am!" But he taught her nothing about himself, until the day she asked, the day of her maturity. "I am good and bad as you," he said. "I left what I believed because there was no one to teach you what you believed." "Will you be punished ?" she asked. "Yes," he said, "I will return to life in a lower state until I have purged this sin." "No," she said, "I will change my belief and become like you so all your teaching will have led me to your way." "Then you will suffer punishment for me," he said, "and that I could not bear. Also, you will lose the precious things I taught you." "How can you call them precious ?" she asked. "You do not believe them."

"I believe them for you," he said. "They have made you into everything I love." "I do not understand," she said; "you are everything I love and nothing I believe." "Then we have a truth," he said, "and maybe not a punishment. I shall have to see. I am close to death, as the priest was to whom I tried to give you."

"If he had taken charge of me," she said, "we would both have died." "Yes," the monk said. "If you had never touched me after your rules, I would have died," she said. "Yes," he said. "Is that how you came to understand the Christ for me?" she asked. "Yes," he said. "And now I have to leave the Christ to you for my own death." "Let me go with you as myself until then." she said. "I'm thin enough to look like boy and girl. I look like you, I talk like you, and in this robe you gave me I can still be everything you taught me." "O, it is good!" he said. "You give me back myself. There is nothing more to hold me."

Reactions to the Gift

What a remarkable thing it is to have your mind wrenched away from the nitty-gritty details of everyday life and be transported in an instant to a level of insight and meaning that warms your heart and puts you in touch with what is truly good. The moment before, you're bogged down in the heaviness of things, and suddenly you are raised up as on eagle's wings. Oh God, how good and great thou art ! For I see you so clearly and feel your presence so tangibly in that good and gracious monk. A moment ago, you seemed so far away, so remote, and now the room is filled with your presence and with your dream. My heart is light, my head is giddy, and all I want to do is cry out: "I love you, God. I love you, Buddhist monk, All people, I love you too. All will be well, all will be well—all manner of things will be well."

What a gift it must be to be able to write like that ! To capture so much truth and goodness—and in less than 800 words too. I wish I could write like that. Francis Sullivan, you are remarkable; thank you very much.

That monk is *awesome.* What a truly good man. He loves like he invented it. I just finished that piece on the *Theology of Presence* a couple of weeks ago, and now I receive a concrete example of that very theology unbidden in the mail. The Spirit seems to be working just fine, thank you. If people ask me what it means to be "present," I can just hand them Sullivan's parable. If the story of the Buddhist monk doesn't make it clear to them, nothing will.

Did you notice, there are no losers in this parable ? That's unusual; usually there is always a "goat." Not this time. The monk, well, what can you say? But the priest...what a good man he was too. I thought I knew where Sullivan was going when he introduced the priest; it sounded a lot like the Good Samaritan story: and the priest walked on by. But no, he fooled me. The priest stopped, and offered to take the child, even though he was himself near death. I think we've got another lover here. And what a warm thing it was to have that loving Catholic priest give the Buddhist monk a final blessing. "May you find peace in life!" And you know, the blessing worked—in the end he did. I wish all priests were like that! And the young woman? Another lover. But then what would you expect? She was raised by the Buddhist monk who loves like he invented it, remember? He sure did it right. She's a marvel. Couldn't quite picture her as a child in my mind, but the image I got of her as a young woman was of someone not unfair of face, but whose inner goodness and loveliness transformed her into a startling beauty. Those two must have been a stunning sight walking together down the road, goodness and beauty radiating from of each of them. Sullivan puts the wisest, most arresting and revelatory line in the whole parable not in the mouth of wisdom and age, the monk or the priest, but in the mouth the young woman: *"You are everything I love, and nothing I believe!"*

You know, it just isn't fair! It isn't fair that so good and loving a man as the Buddhist monk should live out most of his life plagued by fear of punishment. Why do religious institutions do that to people ? Don't they know who God is ? Don't they understand about the Kingdom? What nonsense it all is. "I am not allowed to deal with women young or old. I will lose myself." So he had been taught. And so he believed. Or did he?

On one level he did. That is what caused him all the pain. But on a deeper level, he believed otherwise. Because God was present to him and he to God, he just *knew* that couldn't be right. So he was a house divided, as it were: believing what he had been taught on one level, and deeply knowing on another level that what he had been taught could not possibly be true! How often we're all in that predicament. But this was a truly good and loving man, and so he followed his heart, which was close to God, and put up with the flack he got from his head.

We're all like that to some degree. The church can say all sorts of things, but in our best moments when our hearts are close to God, we know better. It is just that out of fear or for the sake of peace and appearances we often don't have the courage to act on what we know better, the way the monk did.

He knew what love required and pursued it with a vengence, confident not only that God would understand, but that God would want it that way. As so often happens, he was judged harshly by others for trying to do what was truly right and good, and so he found he could not sustain his own life or the child's. So he took counsel with his heart, which was close to God, remember, and decided to live as a Christian to better raise the child. Only when she was mature and self-reliant would he return to the practice of the faith that was his. Is there no end to his love? No limit? He just keeps on loving, no matter what it takes, trusting that his God will understand.

How poignant to read of the Buddhist monk, outwardly living as a Christian, teaching the Christian child her faith, and teaching it with a care and sincerity that would be the envy of many Christians. How his own heart must have wrenched as he taught her "about the judgment...and the place of punished souls." His head must have really given him trouble at that, knowing as he did that he was himself subject to punishment for his "loving" deeds. But still he persisted in doing what love required. Incredible.

The ambiguity of his situation and his concern not to anguish his "daughter" kept him from ever speaking about himself. But she loved him as a father, as indeed he was to her, and wanted to know more about this man who had loved her so and whom she loved above everyone else. So, having reached her majority she made bold to ask him outright. With utter simplicity of spirit, he told her.

Here, in the very moving closing dialogue between them, Sullivan undoubtedly puts forth the central message of his parable. But which is it? There is so much wisdom in this dialogue that one has difficulty deciding which of the many pearls is the one of greatest price.

After revealing to her what he had been doing for many years, she asks him directly, "Will you be punished?" When he tells her that he will, she reacts in a way so characteristic of her loving "father." To prevent punishment from coming down on him, she will give up what she believes for what he believes. Sound familiar? She is indeed her "father's daughter." He taught her well. But it is not so easy. (It never is.) It is a Catch-22 situation. If she becomes Buddhist to save him from punishment, then she is subject to punishment for giving up her faith, the faith he had taught her. If she remains Christian, then he remains subject to punishment. It is a situation in which, out of love, neither can accept the loving gift of the other.

How reminiscent this is of O. Henry's *The Gift of the Magi,* wherein the man sells his watch to buy a set of combs for his wife's beautiful hair, and she cuts her hair and sells it in order to buy him a Christmas watch-fob.

The monk laments that should she give up her faith she would be giving up all the "precious" things he had taught her. At which point she utters the second most arresting line in the parable: *"How can you call them precious? You do not believe them."* It seems like the woman has all the juicy lines in this little scenario. But Sullivan then puts one in the mouth of the monk as he replies: *"I believe them for you; they have made you into everything I love."* But that pearl is immediately upstaged by the woman's reply: *"I do not understand; you are everything I love and nothing I believe."*

That must be close to the central message of Sullivan's parable, because he immediately has the monk say, "Then we have a truth, and maybe not a punishment." Maybe it's a truth, he says, but adds that he will have to wait and see as he is near to death and will soon know one way or the other.

But the young woman will not be put off in the giving of *her* gift of love. In the end she presses hard, confident of the love in her own heart. She reminds the monk that had he obeyed the rules, she would have died. She owes him her very life, as well as her faith. She cannot forget that. Having already proclaimed her love for him, she insists on going with him. "Let me go with you *as myself...*" so I can be with you when you die. In her Buddhist robe, she looks like him, she talks like him, but she can still inwardly be everything Christian which he had taught her.

In her gift of love, she gives the monk back a self he had seemed to abandon years before out of love for her. He rejoices in the gift, and as he approaches his death this good and loving man experiences the blessings of inner peace foretold him in the blessing of the priest.

> Oh God, if only we could be like the young woman, the monk, the priest! If only we could love without fear, without counting the cost. We do sometimes, but not nearly often enough. We long to feel your presence the way they did. We ask your help and your loving patience as we struggle within the narrow confines of our

own lives to look like you, to talk like you, to love like you, and to be "present" to one another as you are present to us. We ask this, Lord, in Jesus name, the Risen and Present One. Amen.

CHAPTER EIGHT

THE "CATHOLIC" ETHOS

The conflicts between the American ethos and the Catholic ethos are real and significant, but it would seem that those conflicts are destined to get worse. They are fated to get worse because of a certain mindless recourse to rules and law on the part of both institutions, the American government and the Roman Catholic church. Each of the institutions, which has formed us from infancy in the dream and faith of our mothers and fathers, seems caught up in a kind of fundamentalist legalism. They seem to have forgotten the basic dream or myth that energized each of them from the beginning. Out of touch with their particular life-giving story, the actions of each seem intent on exacerbating the incompatibilities of being both American and Catholic. Those of us trying to remain faithful to each and true to both are therefore severely compromised. No wonder so many American Catholics are beset with discouragement.

The pope's 1987 visit was chilling, as he rejected change at every turn and suggested that if Americans didn't like it, they were always at liberty to leave the church. And immediately after that, a story from Alaska gave us another portent of things to come. A school principal banned the word "Christmas" from all the school bulletin boards and signs, saying that the law and the principle of the separation of church and state forbade sectarian language in public schools. When challenged, his only response was, "It is the law." Evidently we live in a time when church law and federal law are substituted not only for the basic dream and ethos of each institution, but for common sense as well. When what gives life is judged unlawful, the only possible outcome is death. The death of the republic, and the death of the Catholic church.

One has just to look around to notice all the faces that are missing. It has been said that Christians are to *gather the folks, break the bread,* and *tell the story.* The "story" we are telling these days is not the uplifting one of former times, but the horror story (stories) of a church and a people in crisis. We are preoccupied with the rising dissonance, not only within the American Catholic church, but also within ourselves. When we gather to "break the bread" these days, something seems to be missing. Oh, if we search long and hard enough we can find an uplifting and inspiring liturgy that suits us. Like good Americans we seem to be shopping for liturgies the way we shop for products that enhance our individual selves. But that's not the point. Even when we find one we don't seem to be "present" at it as we once were. Why if one didn't know better, one would think that the individualistic and secular "American" part of us has finally come to full ascendancy causing the "Catholic" part of us to at least recede, if not disappear altogether.

In any case, that's how the present pope seems to see us. And given what we have seen about the current American ethos, it certainly is a more realistic and believable story than that other story he keeps trying to tell *to* us. But one wonders whether a Polish pope closeted with and by Italian cardinals can correctly discern what is going on for "American Catholics" these days. We have come to expect popes not to listen to us. But on his last visit John Paul II showed he won't listen to our bishops either. And the reason he won't listen is because he thinks that he has nothing to learn, since he is convinced that the only way to journey with the Lord as faithful Catholics is "his" way. And "his" way is corroborated by the tradition. But is it ?

A Matter of Conscience

We read in the book of Sirach: "In the beginning, God made man and then left him in the hands of his own counsel" (15:14). This shows that in our tradition the notion of human freedom before God goes way back into the Old Testament. It was put a bit more graphically by the prophet Jeremiah when speaking for the Lord Yahweh:

> Behold the days are coming, says the Lord, when I will make a new convenant with the house of Israel and the house of Judah, not like the covenant which I made with their fathers when I took them by the hand to bring them out of the land of Egypt, my covenant which they broke though I was their husband, says the Lord. But this is the covenant I will make with them, and I will write it upon their hearts, and I will be their God and they will be my people. (31:31-33)

Clearly our God is the God of freedom. This means not only that *God* is free, but also longs to be the God of a *free* people. In fact, God entered our history for no other reason. The whole of the Christian enterprise, in the words of Louis Evely "...represents an initiative on the part of God to communicate himself to humankind. For Christianity is the commitment of God to the liberation of humankind.[17]

The Jews had a real sense of their dignity and understood that Yahweh had called them to freedom, therefore they resented it when the Lord told them that he had come to *really* set them free. We read of their resentment in the eighth chapter of the Gospel of John:

> They answered him, "We are descendants of Abraham and have never been in bondage to anyone. How is it that you say: "You will be *made* free"?

In the Middle Ages, Aquinas put the dignity of human freedom in a way that continues to startle:

> In moral theology we consider man, inasmuch as he is God's image, which is to say: inasmuch as he, like God, is the principle of his own actions, having the power of free choice and the authority to govern himself.[18]

And again:

> All things are subject to the providence of God...but a rational creature is subject to that providence in a more perfect way, because he shares this providence and actually becomes divine providence for himself and for others.[19]

Much more recently, Pius XII put the matter in equally startling terms when he defended the freedom and dignity of the human conscience as follows:

> Conscience is the innermost and secret nucleus in man. It is there that he takes refuge with his spiritual faculties in absolute solitude alone with himself and his God. Conscience is a sanctuary *on the threshold of which all must halt*, even in the case of a child, his father and mother....[20]

And in our own day, in keeping with this constant teaching of the church, the second Vatican Council has affirmed:

> By no human law can the personal dignity and liberty of man be so suitably safeguarded as by the Gospel of Christ. For this gospel announces and proclaims the freedom of the sons of God and repudiates all bondage which ultimately results from sin[21]
>
> The Christian faithful, in common with all other men possess the right not to be hindered in leading their lives in accordance with their conscience.[22]

The tradition is clear, and one can find statements of it in any and every age of the church. The Catholic tradition is one of freedom before God, *not* one of servile obedience. One need not be a Catholic to know that the pontificate of John Paul II has generated a real fear and repressive spirit in the American Catholic community. Bishops, priests, and laity alike, are under increasing pressure from "the top" not to take the freedom part of our Catholic tradition *too* seriously, as the Catholic ethos is interpreted as being essential uniformity with and conformity to past tradition. In the process the longstanding Catholic tradition of freedom is factored out.

Those who quietly accept the present state of affairs still don't know who we are, having no real sense of the dignity and the nobility of our Christian calling. Can you imagine Jesus being afraid the way we are? Certainly he was apprehensive about the suffering he was about to undergo, but this is not the kind of fear we are talking about. Is there any evidence that Jesus was ever afraid of making a mistake? Is there any evidence that Jesus was afraid of following his conscience by standing up, if need be, against the Pharisees? Against Herod? Against Imperial Rome in the person of Pontius Pilate? Is there any evidence that Jesus was afraid to make a personal decision in freedom before God when certain generally valid religious rules did not apply? There is not one shred of evidence of any of this; all the evidence points in the other direction. And if we say, "Yes, but *he* was the Son of God," we simply show that we don't know who *we* are, and have still to understand what God's presence makes of us.

We find it incredible that God really loves us as we are, that God forgives us, and wants us to be truly as free as Jesus, because we are to be the living signs, that is, sacraments, of God's loving presence among us. Because we lack this realization and keep losing our hold on it, we remain timid and unsure of ourselves and think that we must look to others charged with mediating God to us. We give no evidence of being "at home" in God's world. Nor shall we ever feel "at home" here, or there for that matter, unless we at least begin that long, long journey toward authentic freedom. To make that beginning, we must cast off fear, and get a much firmer grasp on the significance of God's presence in our lives.

Those who have not or cannot accept this cornerstone of the Christian tradition have always fallen back on law as their rock and foundation. With its clear-cut regulations, law gives them, if not a sense of their own inestimable worth, at least a sense of order, of discipline, and of the safety and comfort humans normally require. That ought not be underestimated in these chaotic times. God chooses to dwell in us, calls us to freedom, and asks us for our hearts, but fear makes us prefer to embrace the law as our salvation. It is the God who is present, not the Law, which is the source not only of authentic Christian freedom but of revelatory truth as well.

These have always been the Christian alternatives: the God who is present in life and experience, or the law. This whole book is based on the premise that, because of God's living presence in us, experience must take precedence over law. Indeed, as we have already seen, law and authority derive their power and force only when rooted in the faith experiences of people. Lacking this, our obedience becomes at its best formalistic, and at its worst inauthentic. Rejecting the worth of any but experiences like his own, the present pope's call for obedience or departure cannot but be for many a call to inauthenticity, the inauthenticity of complying when your own experience reveals otherwise, and the inauthenticity of leaving when you know in your soul that the Catholic church is where you are called to be.

But perhaps the pope is right. We can't have Americans doing their own thing in the name of expressive individualism and liberty of conscience. That would leave us open to any wind of fancy and make everything all quite arbitrary? Perhaps in the end we do have to choose between being "Catholic" and being "American." Those who insist on having everything according to law may think so. But the demands of Christian conscience are anything but individualistic and arbitrary. To follow one's conscience, for believers, is in no sense the same thing as following one's arbitrary and self-seeking whims. Our God is not a God of confusion, but of peace, and God's Spirit is poured out upon all flesh for the very purpose of leading us out of the isolation and alienation of individualism into that community of love, the church. The doctrine of liberty of conscience asserts human autonomy from *external coercion* but not from the internal consequences of the love of which a person knows him or herself to be the recipient. And that, when you come to think of it, is really the bottom line, isn't it? If I think following my conscience is merely doing what *I* want, then I have failed to realize that due to the presence of God I am not alone in my conscience. As we have already seen, Pius XII makes this expressly clear. God speaks to us, then, not only through our tradition but also through our experiences. No one else may know if I reject the love and invitation of which I am aware, but *I* will know. And if I'm trying seriously to follow God I shall be suffering inwardly from having said no. I will be unable to find that peace which God promised but which only comes from saying "yes."

Conscience as "Catholic"

In keeping with our American predisposition toward individualism (utilitarian and expressive), we tend to think of conscience in terms of the lonely and solitary individual standing nobly and doggedly alone against the forces of compliance no matter what the cost, and we cannot help but admire and reverence such heroism. From the time of the ancient prophets of Israel right up to our own days with the likes of a Daniel Berrigan, a Theresa Kane, and a Mary Agnes Mansour, every nation, every people has had stories, myths, and legends that arise around such people, stories that lift the human spirit and consecrate conscientiousness forever in our hearts. But those same stories dispose us to think of "conscience" exclusively in terms of "individuality," and when we do this we cannot help but create real problems for ourselves. How to relate our conscientious individuality to our life in the community and to communal authority? "Conscience" then becomes code for "opposition to compliance and authority"; "community" code for "what restricts individual freedom"; and "authority" code for "the crushing of non-compliance and individual conscientiousness." Viewed in this way, they are, of course, inevitably opposed.

But this need not be the case. For as the word "conscience" itself indicates, at the heart of human conscience there is also the connectedness, the bondedness, the solidarity of all of humankind. Indeed, in its root meaning "conscience" means "shared knowledge" or "knowledge with another," and it is in virtue of *that* dimension of conscience that no matter how individual it may be, it is at the very same time always at bottom a call and a summons to *all* of humankind. Human conscience is the most fundamental indication that each of us has of not being alone in the universe. The very existence of conscience reveals that no matter how much we might wish to, we cannot "go it alone."

This bears repeating because it is so important. Conscience is an infallible sign of human solidarity, and its existence within us signifies the fact that humankind is to be joined, through the God present in all, in a moral solidarity. If anything in this world of ours is "catholic," it is the human conscience.

This, far more than the Genesis account of "God as lawgiver," is what gives to human conscience its fundamental significance. It is unfortunate, then, that conscience is so often seen in a very limited way as having to do primarily with morality and the human posture vis-a-vis rules and laws. But this was inevitable once we decided to give primacy to the Genesis account of things. The Adam and Eve story, beautiful and insightful as myth or midrash, is simply horrible theology when taken literally because it puts God and humankind into a permanently adversarial relationship. Unfortunately, that is how many Catholics still view God. If one wonders why it is that Jews have traditionally escaped such nonsense, it is because the primary account of their God (Yahweh) arises not from Genesis, but from Exodus. In Exodus, God is not primarily the lawgiver, but the One who lives with them, who is covenanted to them, who enters into dialogue with them, and who eventually liberates them. Put succinctly then, just as the God of Exodus is very different from the God of Genesis, so also an Exodus-conscience is altogether different from a Genesis-conscience. It is *that* difference, which in large measure accounts for the disagreements between Rome and growing numbers of Catholics of the United States.

A Genesis-conscience really isn't "conscientia" at all, because it leaves no room for dialogue regarding the substance of what is a "matter of conscience." That is determined by the law, the rules, by the edicts of authority, any conversation on the matter would only be geared to convincing someone of the truth of what authority maintains. This is conscience on its lowest and most primitive level, if it is conscience at all. It is primitive because it reduces conscience to that inner voice that at moments of moral decision reminds each of us *what* the law is and *that* it must be kept.

Still, a "Genesis conscience" as I have been using that phrase, is not restricted to those who have recourse to law and authority in order to find out what is to be done. That is only its most primitive manifestation. Many people today who shun law and authority are themselves the possessors of a "Genesis-conscience" because, rooted in good old American individualism, they avoid real dialogue with others as well. The essential note of a "Genesis-conscience" is that it rejects all the "con" words and hence fails as *con*-scientia. It neither seeks nor feels the need for: con-sensus, com-munication, cor-roboration, con-firmation, con-currence, com-munality, or con-fession. As such it is only metaphorically con-science. Indeed, when we speak in this way, we can say that only a *good* conscience is authentically "conscience," because only a good conscience can ever become "*con*-scientia," *i.e.*, communally funded by all of humankind. This communal dimension of conscience was captured by Cicero, when he said: "A good conscience calls out to a people, but an evil conscience is agitated in anxious solitude."

By contrast, the Exodus imagery is of a whole people on a journey, living out their lives in the presence of one another, but also in the presence of a God who was covenanted to them and who pledged to share their journey. The great drama of their lives became part of a great ongoing dialogue. And to this day, Jewish faith and theology, even the more Orthodox kind, remain more dialogical than dogmatic.

An "Exodus-conscience," then, is more truly con-scientia, and as such is more appropriate for Christians called to be People of the Kingdom. Ever on a journey, always plagued by the uncertainty of how best to witness God and herald the coming of God's Kingdom, Exodus-Christians feel a real need for contact and solidarity, not only with one another, but with all their sisters and brothers. Walking with God is more a matter of dreaming impossible dreams and mounting the highest ideals, than of "being good," "keeping the commandments," and "doing what one is told." But this does not mean that our faith warrants us to simply "do our own thing" either. For the things that we do in conscience must be such that they call out to all of humankind, presenting an invitation to dialogue and growth.

If conscience is primarily and fundamentally "communal" or "catholic" in character, so too is authority. Not in the sense that authority is required to have a community in the first place, nor in the sense that authority would be meaningless were there no one "under" it, nor even in the sense that authority is a service or ministry for the well being of the governed. No, authority is even more "communal," more "catholic" than that. Authority has its roots in, takes its origin from, and ultimately derives its power from the conscience, consensus, confirmation, corroboration, concurrence, communality, and confession of the community. True of authority in general, this is all the more true when we come to talk of the "Catholic" church, a Christian, Exodus community. Woe to those Catholics who do not heed the words of the Matthean community:

> Jesus then called them together and said: "You know how those who exercise authority among the Gentiles lord it over them, their great ones make their importance felt. *It cannot be like that with you."*

But woe, too, to those who succumb to the typical American temptation "to go it alone." The great contribution that the church can make today is its emphasis on the fact that individuality and human solidarity are not opposites but require each other. It was perhaps necessary at a certain stage in the human journey and in the development of modern society for individuals to declare their independence from oppressive churches, states, and families. But absolute independence is a false ideal. It delivers not the autonomy it promises but the loneliness and vulnerability that are its inevitable fruit.

To be fully human, to be authentically American, to be a person of conscience and to be more than nominally Christian or Catholic *all* require recognition of human bondedness and solidarity. Unmitigated and absolute individualism is sheer madness. That, not mindless obedience, is the good and saving news that the Catholic church has to offer to Americans.

Why Be Catholic?

Every Catholic has his or her own answer to the question, Why be Catholic? Parents strive to formulate a response to give their children some reasoned account of why they should be serious about their Catholic faith. Indeed, it is thought that unless there is some compelling answer to this difficult question, young people will simply walk away from church as a vital element in their lives. Still, with so much at stake, it is interesting to discover that there really is no compelling answer to be given either to our children or to friends who decide to leave the church. Rather than be upset by this fact, perhaps we should try to understand why it is so. In the process we could very well come upon a satisfying if not compelling answer to our question.

We might begin by reflecting on some answers the tradition has given to this question: It is important to be a Catholic because the Catholic church is the one true church; because it has all seven of the sacraments, especially the Mass and Eucharist; because the pope is infallible in matters of faith and morals and the very vicar of Christ on earth; and finally because it is the church founded by Christ who is the Savior of the world and membership in it is the best guarantee of one's eternal salvation.

Such are the triumphal answers we Catholics have been accustomed both to hear and to give in answer to the question, Why be Catholic? But a moment's reflection reveals that however important those reasons may be, they are not the essential elements that make the church "Catholic." To better see the "Catholic" ethos, it might help to consider what is characteristically "Protestant" on the assumption that it will be diametrically opposed to what is truly "Catholic."

It must be said that what characterizes Protestantism through its venerable history is *division*. Not diversity simply, because despite outward appearances Catholics are an extremely diverse lot themselves, *but diversity that "divides."* The fact is that Protestants are really much more homogeneous than Catholics. This homogeneity is purchased at the price of division. This is their tradition; this is their history. If several people don't like what the minister says, they break off with others of like mind and form their own church or congregation. So it is that Protestantism is composed of a great multiplicity of diverse communions, each of which is far more homogeneous than is the Catholic church. The genius of the liberty to break off and form new communities is built into the Protestant ethos.

It is quite otherwise with Catholics. As the name suggests, we have an entirely different orientation. "Catholic" means "universal," and the genius of the Catholic ethos is that despite diversity *everyone* is in, *everyone* is part of us. The Catholic dream of universality is not a dream of homogeneity without diversity. Far from it. The Catholic dream is to have unity with diversity—a truly universal communion. It is not out of the question for us to dream of the day when there would be Buddhist Catholics, Methodist Catholics, Lutheran Catholics, Bahai Catholics, etc. For Catholics, then, religious liberty is not seen primarily as the freedom to leave and separate, *but the freedom to remain while disagreeing.* Unfortunately, that dream down through the centuries has been skewered by attempts to interpret the Catholic ethos as one of total uniformity rather than as unity in diversity. And whenever in our history popes have waged a battle for complete submission to orthodoxy, they have betrayed the basic Catholic dream and have unwittingly adopted a divisive perspective.

Vatican II crystallized and proclaimed this "catholic" dream more eloquently than had ever been done previously in the history of the Roman church. But as the awareness grew that this proclamation of the solidarity of all of humankind under God made it more and more difficult to give satisfactory answers to the question, "Why be Catholic?" many in high places in the church began to have second thoughts. We seem to be embarking on a very reactionary time in the church as Pope John Paul II seeks to interpret the traditional Catholic ethos in a particularly divisive way. His urgings of absolute orthodoxy, his silencing of dissent first by women and now by theologians, his heavy-handed treatment of the best of our bishops has shocked and dismayed American Catholics, who were so energized by the dream of the Council.

The temptation of many is to leave in the name of religious freedom. *But this is precisely the wrong time to leave the Catholic church.* If ever there was a time to stay or even come into the church it is now. Now is *not* the time to leave because, despite appearances, the Roman Catholic church is on the verge of becoming for the first time in its history truly "catholic." What we are witnessing in the present upheaval is the death of the "Roman" Catholic church and the birth of a whole new "catholic" reality. The present repressions are the last acts of desperation, attempting to abort the new life that is aborning.

Why be Catholic? Because however skewered and under attack the dream of universality and human solidarity may at present be, that dream is the essential meaning of being Catholic; it is kept alive, even when it is not lived out, only in the Catholic church. In a world divided by hatred and bigotry, by war and rumors of war, there is only one institution that continues to foster and advance the dream. *The Catholic ethos is the ethos of our time.* Its dream of peaceful solidarity amid diversity is precisely what the world needs as its technology ends the isolation and dividedness of humankind and ushers in the global village. To leave the church because of disagreement or diversity simply delays the day of that hope-filled future.

Why be Catholic? Because at its best, the Catholic church is the only institution that on its own principles not only can but must, in order to keep faith with its very nature and history, proclaim what other religious institutions find so difficult to accept: *"You're one of us.* You haven't been a member? That's all right; you see, *It really doesn't matter."*

If we give heed to our lives, and live long enough, we come to understand the things that eluded us earlier because of our youth and the dogmatic posture of our religious teachers. We come to know how the Yahweh-God works in the world, and we come to appreciate the dream of the Kingdom, God's commitment to and presence in *all* of humankind. The divisions melt away and we finally understand the meaning of ancient Israel's claim: "Hear O Israel, the Lord our God is one." Once our experiences bring us to this point, we can no longer be parochial. We can no longer say with conviction that one must be a Catholic. Rather, we rejoice in our own Catholicism, for we see it at its best, incarnating what the God of life has finally revealed to us in our experience, what in fact is revealed by God's presence in *all* of humankind: *It really doesn't matter.*

Why be Catholic? Finally, because for those of us who are, these are our roots, and that's who we are, that's our tradition. Where else could we go? Because if in the end it really doesn't matter to which church I belong but rather how well I witness the loving presence of God to all of humankind, then I am perfectly at liberty to be who and what I am. And for some of us, that means remaining and becoming *better* and more authentic "Catholics."

What Does Matter?

It would be terrible if we ended this book mindlessly repeating the slogan: *It really doesn't matter.* Not that the slogan is wrong, quite the contrary, but we had better be certain we understand just what that word "it" means in our slogan. Many may think we're saying that nothing matters, but our parable about the Buddhist monk points to something different. There are many things that really matter, and we know it. It is just that many of us have lived long enough, and journeyed far enough, all the while reflecting on our lives, that we can finally distinguish more clearly what matters from what doesn't.

Now the "it" in *It really doesn't matter* refers to all those things that human ingenuity has devised to divide people from one another. With regard to religion, these divisive "human" inventions are actually attributed to God and issue in such things as: "sectarianism," "parochialism," and "triumphalism." For example, as we have seen, *we* tell the story that somehow God was revealed in a special way to Israel. Not true. From the start, God was present and revealing to *all* of humankind. This is God's nature! This is what it means to be Spirit. It is not that God somehow favored Israel with a gift not given to others, but rather that it was ancient Israel that first caught on, that first came to the realization that God does not dwell in some far-off place, but with humankind.

In the civil order, crushing divisions arise from "nationalism." In the social and economic order the divisions are made according to wealth, prestige, and power, and go by the names: "racism," "sexism," and "discrimination" of all sorts. When we proclaim and shout, *"It really doesn't matter,"* we are expressing the fact that such divisions within the human race are the only heresy; a human solidarity based on God's presence in and to all of humankind and on our own loving and salvific "presence" to one another is ultimately the only thing that really matters.

But just to make this claim is precisely to express the essential genius of what it means to be American as well as the essential dynamic, as we have seen, of Catholicism. What I am suggesting, then, is this: Not only is there no inherent contradiction in one's being *both* American *and* Catholic, but Catholicism is, in the order of faith/religion, precisely what the American ethos and dream (at their best) are in the secular order. Individualism may be at present the American condition; it is too mean and divisive to be the American dream. To a world sorely divided along national, ethnic, and racial lines, the American ethos celebrates ethnic and racial diversity and clearly says these things really don't matter. To a world torn asunder along religious, doctrinal, and theological lines, the Catholic ethos insists on the basic solidarity, amid the diversity, between God and humankind and hence between all of God's children as well.

Bellah and company identify "individualism" as *the* American character trait, but if we interpret this solely in terms of its "utilitarian" and "expressive" manifestations, we find, as they did, that it conflicts not only with faith but with any meaningful human solidarity. But the word "individual" can also mean what cannot be divided, and we might take the liberty of applying this not only to our personal lives, but to the human family as a whole. In that extended sense, Emma Lazarus's words at the base of the Statue of Liberty capture best the truer and more authentic American ethos:

> Give me your tired, your poor,
> Your huddled masses yearning to be free,
> The wretched refuse of your teeming shore.
> Send these, the homeless, tempest-tost to me.
> I lift my lamp beside the golden door !

You are poor—it doesn't matter. You are homeless—it doesn't matter. You are Irish—it doesn't matter. You are Slavic—it doesn't matter. You are Native American—it doesn't matter. You are Black—it doesn't matter. You are Asian—it doesn't matter. You are woman—it doesn't matter. You are powerless—it doesn't matter. And the reason it doesn't matter is because you are one with us, and we with you! And because we are one with you, we shall do everything we can to help you end your poverty, your homelessness, and your powerlessness.

Of course, this same dream is kept alive in the Catholic church. While the pope acts in a peculiarly divisive way when handing out his theology, he recently acted as a truly "catholic" pope. He gathered all the religious leaders of the world at Assisi to pray for peace, and called on all combatants the world over to honor a one day cease-fire. The press labeled the effort a failure, because a universal cease-fire did not happen. But the event was an eminently "Catholic" success. You're Buddhist—it doesn't matter. You're Hindu—it doesn't matter.

You're Anglican—it doesn't matter. You're Baptist—it doesn't matter. You're Bahai—it doesn't matter. And the reason it doesn't matter is because God dwells in you and your people, and God dwells in me and my people, which makes us all one! And while it is possible that when Pope John Paul II had all those religious leaders in Assisi he was privately thinking of how he could convert them all to the one "true" church, the fact is the event itself symbolized future and witnessed against all the religious divisions that plague our planet.

It is unfortunate that many think that when the pope puts forth his traditional moral teachings he is "being truly Catholic," and when he consorts with those of other faiths he is merely "being ecumenical." As I have tried to show, the reverse is true. But take heart, because the pope does have a "Catholic" side to him, and when he acts out of that ethos, he is pope not just of Catholics, but of all of humankind.

So now we come to the end of our journey, strengthened, it is hoped, in the vision of what it really means to be Catholic and American, and what it is that really matters. The church of our youth is passing, and a whole new "catholic" reality is aborning. And at its birth we cannot be discouraged. For what is coming to be in our very midst is the fruit of the Present One. Rejoice, and let us pledge ourselves in the time we have left to be more "Catholic" and more "American" than we have ever been before. Let us pray for the courage to be ever more open, hospitable, sharing, and "present" to our world.

> O God, Creator and Nurturer of All, we ask for new "habits of heart." We wish to be done with all those things that divide us from one another and from you. But our self-centeredness runs deep. So we know we cannot make the transformation on our own. We therefore ask that you surround us with others who share the dream, that in communion with them we may make real progress toward the goal. We ask your blessing for the task at hand - in the name of Jesus, our God and Brother—Who leads us on the way. Amen.

QUESTIONS FOR REFLECTION AND DISCUSSION

INTRODUCTION

1. Eugene Kennedy, in his one-man play *I Would Be Called John,* puts these words in the mouth of Pope John XXIII: "Let me tell you, of all the confessions I have listened to, I have not heard sin nearly so much as I have heard discouragement. Discouragement of themselves, and of life. *Discouragement is what truly kills people.* It is not their failings. No, I don't think most people are great sinners."

What are your thoughts about this? What is discouragement anyway? Especially discouragement of life itself? Have you ever experienced it?

2. Westley seems to think that American Catholics these days are discouraged. What do you think? About what are the Catholics you know most discouraged?

3. Being both American and Catholic used to be an unbeatable combination. As Westley says, "we are citizens of the greatest nation on the earth, and members of the one *true* church. An unbeatable combination. And so we walked this earth as if we owned it, like a race of giants, heads held high, confident in our demeanor and bearing, making our superiority felt, aware that children of a lesser god would give anything to be in our shoes."

a) Do you remember thinking in this way? Share your feelings and some of your experiences about this former time.

b) Obviously, we can no longer think this way. What happened? Would you like to return to those "glory" days? Why? Why not?

4. What pains you most these days about America? About the Catholic church? About yourself?

Discovering the Centrality of "Presence"

1. You will get a chance to discuss the significance of Westley's one-liner in the dialogue questions for Chapter One. But if you have some things you want to say about it now, this is the place to do it.

2. Any reactions to Westley's story about having a moment of insight, a transforming moment? Have you ever had such an experience?

CHAPTER ONE: A THEOLOGY OF PRESENCE

I. The One-Liner

"I have called you to live out your lives in the 'presence' of one another, and I pledge Myself to live out My life in 'your' presence."

1. Westley makes some pretty extravagant claims for his precious little one-liner. For example:

a) It is the sum of Christian theology....

b) It is the heart and essence of Christianity....

c) It is all the theology he knows....

d) It is all the theology there is....

Now really! What do you make of such claims? Do you see in the one-liner what Westley apparently sees there? What is it you see?

2. Perhaps the meaning of the line could be better seen and understood if one breaks it down into its component parts. Each phrase must be important since brevity was what Westley was after. So each phrase contributes something essential, otherwise it would have been omitted. Share your "deepest" understanding of each of the following phrases:

a) I have called you...

b) ...to live out your lives...

c) ...in the presence of one another...

d) ...and pledge Myself...

f) ...to live out *my* life...

g) ...in *your* presence.

3. What difference does it make to say that Israel was not so much chosen by God from among the nations, as that they were the first to recognize a revelation that was being given to all? And even if it makes a difference for Jews, what possible difference could this make for Catholics? Explain.

II. The Mystery of Presence

1. Presence is said to be both the nature and the vocation of "spirit," only "spirit" can be present. What does it mean to be "present" to another? How can you tell if someone is not "present" to you? How does it make you feel? Conversely, share an experience when someone was truly present to you. Describe what it felt like, and what effect it had on you.

2. Spirituality is sometimes described in ways that give the impression of fleeing from the world. It is claimed here that "presence" is the heart of any genuine spirituality, and that faith calls us not to flee the world but to be truly "present" to it. From your own experience describe what a spirituality *without* presence might look like. What does it mean to be "present" to the world? Are you?

III. What It Means to Be "Incarnate Spirit"

1. The Platonic account of human nature suggests that we are "imprisoned spirits" using a body. Aquinas says rather that we are "incarnate spirits" who in some way **are** our bodies. From the perspective of Christian faith, which is the more appropriate account and why? What difference does it really make?

2. Most Christians, according to Westley, are Platonists who have an overspiritualized view of human life and Christian faith and end up misunderstanding the role of matter/body in human life. Far from being a hindrance to spirit, matter/body is humankind's way of reaching spiritual perfection. In the light of all this comment on each of the following:

a) "The role of the body is to enable a human being to do the work of spirit, which is presence."

b) "If we would truly know and love one another, if we would know and love God we must understand we can do neither without a body."

c) "The human body is not only a biological wonder, it is a spiritual marvel as well." Give some examples from your own life and experience of:

i) The human face as instrument of spirit....
ii) The human voice as instrument of spirit....
iii) The human hand as instrument of spirit....

4. Undoubtedly, one of the most startling conclusions to flow from Aquinas's vision of humans as "incarnate spirits" is that when it comes to the work of the Kingdom, the work of love, and any of their ministries, we have only two things with which to accomplish our mission, i.e., our words and our physical presence. Comment on the following:

a) It is interesting to consider the claim that Jesus, too, had only these two things to do his salvific work. It might prove instructive to read the gospel stories of Jesus from this particular perspective. Choose a gospel passage which you think demonstrates this truth most clearly. Share your understanding of the passage with the group.

b) These same two things are said to be the only things we have to mediate God's unconditional love of God to one another and to have what the tradition calls a "spirituality." Describe what sort of "spirituality" you are practicing at the present time, and then show either how words and physical presence are or are not integral to it.

IV. Conclusion

1. "A rigid spiritualism has plagued the Christian faith throughout its history. Someone is always trying to overspiritualize the faith enterprise out of fear. This fear causes them, following the lead of Plato and the ancient Stoics, to set up two worlds—one of body and matter, and the other of soul and spirit. But there is only *one* God. And there is only **one** world. In fact there is only one reality—*Spirit in the World*, to use Karl Rahner's happy phrase."

a)What do you make of the claim that *there is only one reality* and that it is *Spirit in the World*?

b)If that is so, then it follows that:

i) God = Spirit in the World
ii) Human Beings = Spirit in the World
iii) All the rest of Creation = Spirit in the World
What does this tell you about "incarnation" as the central truth of faith?

2.Comment on the following:

"So we should stop talking about the 'spiritual' life. We should talk rather about 'life' and of our God who is incarnate there, revealing to us in our experience all we need to know in order to, like God, *be truly present* to one another and to our world."

CHAPTER TWO: SEX AND THE CONTEMPORARY FAMILY

I. The Family Crucible

"Warning: Families Can Be Dangerous to Your Health"

1. Were you offended by Westley's account of family life? Did it seem too pessimistic to you? What is your assessment of the situation? From your own family experience, which of the following best describes your family:

a) crucible b) war zone c) haven d) sanctuary
e) motel/laudromat f) where the partying never ends
g) where "words" and "physical presence" witness the Kingdom h) where I feel God's "presence" i) other—please specify.

2. "The tone of the nuclear age is just the final and ultimate expression of what has been at the heart of human families from the beginning, *conflict*. Families are being torn apart because its members foster the natural conflict-mechanisms within the family while at the same time resisting or abusing its natural bonding-mechanisms."

a) From your own familial experience list the *natural conflict-mechanisms* which you see as part of every family.

Which ones are most operative in your own family?

b)From your own familial experience list the *natural bonding-mechanisms* which you see as part of every family. Is sex a natural bonding or conflict mechanism in your family? Explain.

3. If your family doesn't match the high ideals so often held up, what has accounted for this in your judgment? How would you "name" the central issue that is the source of most of the difficulties? Is it one of the four mentioned below or is it another one? (Drugs, alcohol, etc. are not "central" issues but flow from one of the "central" ones.)

Westley names four such "central" issues: "At the heart of every human family is the basic *clash of wills*, the *conflict of differing value systems*, the *struggle between dependence and autonomy*, and most significantly, the *challenge of relating sexually*."

4. When we work for peace and justice, we usually think of things in global or national terms, but the fact of the matter is there is little peace and justice in the land because there is so little peace and justice in the family. Evidently, we're so busy being "loving" in our families that there is no "justice" there, and so there is no "peace" either. Any comments?

5. What changes in your own family would have to be made if family members committed themselves to treating each other justly? Be specific.

6. Doesn't Westley overstate the case when he claims that the Catholic church is inadvertently "anti-family" because of its inability to speak meaningfully (i.e., non-Platonically) about the meaning of sex in family life?

II. The Meaning of Human Sexuality

A. The Culture's Story on Sex

1. In 1970 Professor Robert Tyler wrote: "Let us agree that *marriage is impossible.* It has *always* been an impossible institution. In all its many forms, it has clamped some kind of social control on sex to make fun and games serve such stuffy values as child-rearing, the inheritance of wealth, or the

transmission of social status and tradition. But sex has always burst the boundaries! *American marriage has been especially impossible.* From the beginning Americans frowned on all those extra-marital sports discovered by older and wiser cultures to make the institution livable. The strain in American marriage, of course, has been terrific. In the early phases of our present sexual revolution after World War I, the cracks in the old, crumbling edifice were papered over by well-meaning romantics who wrote marriage manuals. By now attempts to save the institution have become pretty desperate. Already one can see the future taking shape in the experiments of the present college-age generation, which has apparently decided to deal with the institution by ignoring it as an anachronism and hypocrisy." ("The Two-Marriage, Revolving Mate, Generation Bridging Plan to Save Marriage," *The Humanist*, Nov./Dec. 1970)

Almost twenty years later, Tyler's words seem almost prophetic, even though offensive. What are your reactions?

2. Andrew Greeley once wrote that marriage is in reality more "...a state of armed, lustful, coexistence" than an experience of love and intimacy. Indeed, he went on to add: "It is the burden of intimacy which crushes the physical attractiveness of marriage." Any reactions to this?

3. Westley seems to think that women have (or at least had until recently) a special insight into the meaning of *human* sexuality. Isn't that a rather naive and sexist view? He laments that women are more and more thinking like men these days, but haven't men and women always thought alike about sex?

4. We hear a lot these days about "nuclear free zones." Given the way the American culture fills the air with pornography, wouldn't it be wise for us to establish "pornographic free zones," where people could gather and be free of oppressive sexual stimuli? Any comments or suggestions?

II. The Catholic Church's Story on Sex

1. Does the institutional church's stand on the essential nature of openness to procreation *in each and every sexual act* have any credibility with you? Why? Why not?

2. Westley says: "It does not help to call such a teaching "traditional," meaning it has been taught for a long time, for it has been wrong for exactly that same amount of time." Evidently, in order to be traditional, something must not only have been taught for a long time, it must also have been right all that while too. Any comments?

3. In sexual matters, Westley says that lay people; "like children, seem to wait to be told, told by those who really know. But the fact is, those who claim really to know, don't." Any comments?

a) Of those who claim to know, Pope John Paul II seems to be obsessed with the need to set the world straight on sex. What are your reactions to his many statements on the matter since he became pope? Does talking the way he does help or hurt?

b) "It is time for sexually active believers to proclaim in God's name, and without fear, what they have learned in bed, confident that it is, when communally funded, as authoritative as any episcopal letter or papal encyclical." Isn't this an outrageous statement? If not, why not?

i) What have you learned "in bed?"

ii) How do you go about discerning whether what you learned "in bed" is true or not? In order for it to be authoritative it must be "communally funded." What does this mean to you?

4. Comment on the thought that lived sexual experience clearly, directly, and consistently contradicts what the hierarchical church teaches about sex. Share how you learned the church's position was wrong-headed, and how you came to change your own conscience on the matter.

III. "Having Sex" vs. "Making Love"

1. "Human sex is primarily *relational*, having little or nothing to do with biological procreation, having everything to do with human bonding." If this claim is to be taken seriously, by Westley's own principles it must be "communally funded." Contribute to that communal funding by sharing your own experiences in the matter. Do they support Westley's claim or not?

2. The church says that these two functions cannot be separated nor can one be given precedence over the other. Is that what your experience tells you? What do you say?

3. Westley makes much of the fact that human language has come to describe human sexual intercourse as "making love." Is this just a euphemism or is there a reality that this kind of language is trying to get at?

4. Becoming sexually aroused may well be in the genes (and in the hormones), but "making love" must be learned. How are the young to learn it? What would you say to a young person who asked you about the meaning of sex?

IV. What It's Like to "Make Love"

1.What comes to your mind when you see the following two statements juxtaposed?

a) Human sexual intercourse is love-making.

b) God is Love.

2. When one manages to have his or her sexual activity "make-love" he or she cannot help but recognize it, Westley says, because of the following signs. Share your thoughts and experiences about each of them.

a) One finally understands what human sexual relations are really all about. They are about the work of presence, the work of love.

b) One feels in solidarity with the beneficent presence that transcends and yet dwells in our world.

c) One feels gifted and graced.

d) One, for however briefly, feels no need to dominate, no need to assert oneself, no need to manipulate, so delicious is the taste of being and of being loved.

e) One feels forgiving and forgiven, at one with God and all of humankind, face to face with not only what is truly good, but with the Goodness that is the hidden source of every other good.

f) One feels oneself to be in a truly saving place and thinks to oneself: "This surely must be what salvation is all about!"

g) One is energized, feels better able to love, and finds oneself more generous, more giving, more open, and less self-conscious.

Does this list of "signs" speak to you? How would you put this experience into your own words?

3. From your own experience, and in your own words, say what you understand Westley to mean when he says "Sexual activity (for humans) is spirituality." And that "To makes one's sexual activity love-making is the most difficult of the spiritual arts." Why?

V. The American Family in Crisis

1. Face it, families have a "sexual" center. As Virginia Satir says: "The marital relationship is the axis around which all other family relationships are formed." We don't like to admit this, especially when thinking of our own families of origin. As an observer, how would you judge the sex life of your parents to have gone? Did they ever talk to you about it? What did they say? What effect did/does it have on you?

2. How does your sex life affect your own family? Relations with your spouse, relations with the children? Does your own experience tend to corroborate the centrality of sex in family life? Explain.

3. Other forces erode the family at its periphery, but the insane and dehumanizing cultural view of sex and the over-spiritualized view of sex on the part of some religions strike at its heart. Families will remain at risk until the love-making and bonding powers of human sex are prized and practiced.

Share how the cultural view of sex affects your relations with your spouse and thus affects your family.

Share how the Catholic church's view of sex affects or affected your relations with your spouse and thus with the rest of the family as well.

4. What was your reaction to the discovery of family therapists that in a very large percent of cases, troubled teenagers are really reacting to the troubled marital relations of their

parents? That seems like scapegoating, doesn't it? Still, what if it is true? What does your experience reveal to you on this matter?

CHAPTER THREE: EXPERIENCE AS AUTHORITY

I. The Infallibility Issue

1. When the church proclaims that popes are infallible in matters of faith and morals, what does that mean to you? Does it have any effect on what *you* believe? How do you incorporate the doctrine of infallibility into your own faith life?

2. Westley says that so long as Catholics remember how John XXIII "poped," they will find it difficult to accept any other kind. What do you make of that statement?

3. Westley claims that as the infallibility of the pope has become central to Catholic faith, the role of the common consensus of believers has been significantly diminished. From your own perspective, share what this statement means to you and whether you think it is correct or not.

II. Lived Experience as Revelatory

1. The claim is often made that "experience is the best teacher." Is this true even in the realm of faith? It would seem not, since the truths of faith have been handed down to us by the authoritative teaching of others. Experience seems to be irrelevant in such matters. Any thoughts?

2. On the other hand, what authority proclaims arose out of the *lived experience* of Jews and early Christians, so experience was not always irrelevant to the truths of faith. It is just that after centuries of accumulation, it is "present" experience that has been ruled out in favor of prior experience. So we need an "infallible" pope to tell us what to believe. Ruling out "present" experience seems to be truly wrong-headed. What do you think? Give examples of some things of faith on which "present" experience seems closer to the truth than the traditional position as far as you're concerned.

3. Westley writes: "God's presence at our very center makes of *our lives* revelation, *i.e.,* sacred shrines from which we may, if only we avail ourselves of the opportunity, learn life's deepest truths. So true is that, that as we have now come to understand the Bible is itself divine revelation precisely because it arose from the ancient Hebrews' and early Christians' encounter with the Living God in their lives. Whenever we lose sight of this fact, we cannot help but rob life of its revelatory dimension placing our primary trust elsewhere, i.e., in sacred books like the Bible, or sacred people like the pope.

Do you ever think of your "life" as a *font of revelation?* Explain.

What else in this passage caught your attention and started you thinking in a new direction?

4. Those in authority can say what they will, but what they say is judged by "adults" and not simply accepted because it was said with authority. Do you feel confident enough of your own experience to say you can tell the difference between what *is* and what isn't only opinion?

III. The Pope

1. Not every kind of pope-ing is in accord with the dream of the Kingdom. As you understand "the coming of the Kingdom," what kind of pope-ing does it seem to require? Or, more concretely, what was it about John XXIII's pope-ing that makes it a model of how popes should exercise their charge?

2. "Whatever authority popes may come to have, stems more from their *presence* than from their *office.*" What does this statement mean to you?

3. Comment on the following: "Pope-ing, like being a Christian, is really an exercise in salvific presence."

Say how this means that even popes have norms by which their authority is measured. What is salvation anyway? (Isn't the phrase "salvific presence" really redundant because "presence" cannot but be "salvific"?)

4. What do you make of Westley's claim that authority is

really "given" and not "had"? Is it true? Give some supporting evidence from your own experience.

IV. The Bible

1. Give some examples not found in this book of when Scripture at least seems to contradict itself. What do you make of that?

2. Westley thinks that such contradictions show that the Bible is not itself the "Word of God," but is rather a human word proclaimed and written in response to God's presence. How does this view strike you? What difference does it make?

3. What would it mean to say that "life" has more authority than the Bible? What would it mean to say that the Bible has more authority than life?

4. Westley takes both the Bible and the pope as having an authority derived from life or experience. This is because life and experience are God-filled, and God is the *ultimate* authority.

What are the consequences of taking the "God of Life" as the ultimate authority? What kind of a church would we have if we did this?

V. The Authority Issue

1. As far as you are concerned in what human institutions or persons does divine authority reside? Many persons, writings and institutions claim divine authority (Hitler, Idi Amin, Khomeni, Kadafy, etc.). How does one determine whether these are the claims of fanatics or whether divine authority *actually* resides there?

2. A major division among Catholics centers on to what they attribute God's primary authority, life, the Bible, the church, the magisterium, or the pope. Where are you? What is it like living in the same church with others who find God's primary authority elsewhere than you do?

3. "If you don't give absolute obedience to the pope and the

magisterium there is a name for you. The name is Protestant." What are your thoughts about saying it's total acceptance and total obedience or nothing for Catholics?

4. Westley speaks of "faithful dissent" as opposed to a dissent that rends the very fabric of the believing community. Is that a viable distinction? Doesn't *all* dissent rend the fabric of the believing community?

VI. Authority: As We First Came to Know It

1. Is there any difference in the way authority is exercised in the world and in secular institutions and the way it is exercised within the church? Should there be?

2. Each of us has had an experience of "faithful dissent" either by a family member, a friend, a priest, a nun, a teacher, which profoundly affected our lives and contributed mightily to our faith. Share the story of such an experience.

VII. Authority: As We Now Understand It

1. "What passes for authority in other spheres fails as authority in the realm of faith." What evidence do you have for the truth of this statement? For its falsity?

2. Isn't it the task of the church to tell its members what to believe and what to think on important issues? One gets the impression that Westley thinks it is the members who should tell the hierarchical church what to proclaim. Surely that's totally inverted, isn't it?

3. What are your reactions to Westley's account of how authority works in his life? Does it really, as he says, work that way in yours too?

a) Westley seems to have a "hang-up" with authority, wouldn't you say? Who does he think he is, anyway?

b) Where did Jesus' authority come from? (Before you simply say he was the Son of God and nothing more need be said, recall that most of the people who listened to him didn't know that was the case.)

CHAPTER FOUR: SALVATION FOR INCARNATE SPIRITS

I. The Traditional View of Salvation

1. When you think of the "end of the world," what comes to mind? How do you react to the thought that the material world isn't going to go up in smoke and fire, but will be transformed at the end into the Kingdom?

2. Comment on the following: "Misunderstanding the role of the human body in the work of spirit, we could not help but also misunderstand the role and significance of the material world in the economy of salvation." What is the salvific significance of the material world we live in?

3. What do you make of the suggestion that our pagan and secular culture has a vested interest in keeping believers pursuing an "other worldly" salvation? What's in it for the culture if Christians keep working for heaven?

4. What are your reactions to the claim that "religious liberty" in the United States is predicated on the premise that religion not have an impact on this world, but concern itself only with the next? Any examples of this?

5. Give some examples from your own experience of how the Catholic church is "integrated" into the American system. Give some examples that show that in some areas, at least, it is not integrated.

6. Isn't it a good thing that the churches concern themselves with "salvation"? Why is Westley against describing the task of the church that way?

II. Salvation and Ancient Israel

1. Twenty-five years after Vatican II, the Catholic church seems to be saying that we must have a special interest and concern for the poor. This sounds very much like what was said in ancient Israel. Why is this important? What do you make of the fact that this part of our tradition, which goes all the way back to the prophets of Israel, seems to have been somewhat ignored by lay Catholics in favor of a "personal" salvation?

2. According to Westley, "...the quality of human life on this earth is integral to any notion of salvation." How so? Is this really our deepest tradition? When did you come to recognize that salvation was not exclusively some "other worldly" event?

III. The Indeterminateness of the Early Christian View

1.The claim is made that unlike many other essential dogmas of Christian/Catholic faith, there is a multiplicity of understandings possible regarding the meaning of "salvation."

2. From your own education and background, make a list of the various different ways you have heard that truth thematized. Then share your list with the group, and make some brief comments about each of the items on your list.

3. Comment on this text of St. Paul:

"All this has been done by God, who has reconciled us to himself through Christ and has given us the ministry of reconciliation. I mean that God, in Christ was reconciling the world to himself, not counting humankind's transgressions against them, and that he has entrusted the message of reconciliation to us. This makes us ambassadors for Christ, God as it were appealing through us." (2 Corinthians 5:18-20)

4. What do you take the word "reconciliation" to mean in this passage? Explain.

IV. Understanding the Murder of Jesus

1. What story do you tell yourself when *you* are trying to explain what part the "murder of Jesus" had in God's plan of salvation/reconciliation, God's plan of atonement?

2. Read the four Servant of the Lord oracles in the book of Isaiah: 42:1-4; 49:1-7; 50:4-11 and 52:13-53:12. What themes here best express what you were taught about salvation? What do you see there now that you didn't see before?

V. Three Christian Theories of Atonement

1. Have someone give a summary of the major points in the *Classical* theory of atonement of the Greek Fathers. What

about this view is objectionable and grossly primitive? What about this view is still significant for us today? Explain.

2. The *Latin* view seems so legalistic, and gets involved in the problem of just "satisfaction" for sin. Is this an improvement over the classical view? What are its strengths? What are its weaknesses? Does it still speak to you today?

3. Make as good a case as you can for the *subjective* view. What is its major strength? Do you agree that this view seems to make sin and alienation almost trivial? Explain.

VI. Salvation: A Psychological Perspective

1. Have you or anyone in your family been in counseling? What was the experience like? Did you find it difficult and awkward, or did you find it helpful and salvific? What are your reactions to the claim that in the contemporary world more and more people look to therapists rather than to the churches for saving help?

2. "Each person needs a 'place' where the fragments and loose ends of life can be collected, experienced and treated with care, a place of salvation." This is so true as to be trivial. But notice the emphasis on the word "place." What does that say to you? Where is your "place of salvation"?

3. "It is in the counseling session, rather than in the churches, that many come to recognize those elements of salvation that we have been discussing." Share how you or someone you know found the elements of "salvation" in therapy.

4. Comment on this description of "salvation" by Parker Palmer:

"To be saved, to be made whole, is to realize that we are in the contradictions, that the contradictions are in us, and that all of it is held together by a 'hidden wholeness.' It is to be able to anywhere with anyone, in freedom and in love."

VII. Conclusion

This has been a difficult chapter. What did you get out of

it? How did it affect your thinking about "salvation"? How did it affect your life? What do you see now that you didn't before?

CHAPTER FIVE: COMMUNITY: THE SAVING PLACE

I. Why Suddenly "Community"?

1. What has been your reaction to increased pressure for Catholics to become/be in community? What reservations or resistances do you find to this within yourself? Explain.

2. Share your most memorable experience of "community." What makes it so memorable for you?

3. "There seem to be only two directions for humankind to move in. Either toward community, or toward Babel." Comment on this remark, sharing from your own experience the community dimensions and the Babel dimensions of your life.

4. What does one say to a person who says: "I'm a loner, I like my independence, I don't need community. I just want to be left alone so I can do my own thing with God"?

5. In the old days, what did the expression "living in sin" mean to you? Westley wants to give this expression a new meaning. What does he mean by "living in sin"? Any reactions.

6. Comment on the following:

"We are going to have to be willing to place ourselves in situations and circumstances that allow us to give up our assertive and aggressive ways and learn the lessons of community, intimacy and solidarity. Only thus can we stop 'living in sin.'"

II. The Christian Churches and Community

1. If reconciliation is the primary ministry of the Christian churches, how goes it among themselves? They can hardly witness the message of reconciliation if they are divided against each other. How are things between the Christian churches of your neighborhood? Who stands more in the way of real and effective reconciliation between them—their leaders, or their people? Explain.

2. Are there any non-Christian churches in your area? Where do they fit in? What role do they have in God's work of reconciliation? How are their relations with the Christian churches? How do you feel about Jews? Moslems? Buddhists? Hindu? etc.

3. What do you make of Matthew 5:23? And of the claim that nothing, not even worship of God, takes precedence over reconciliation?

4. What does Westley mean when he says that "sectarianism is the only heresy"? After you decide what he might mean, do you think that what is said is true or not? Explain.

5. Comment on the line from Martin Buber: "We expect a theophany of which we know nothing but the place. And the place? The place is called *community*."

6. Share a theophany from your own community. (What is a theophany anyway? How can you be sure that what you experienced was really a theophany?)

III. Community: End or Means?

1. Westley distinguishes "unions of convenience" from community. What is a "union of convenience"? Why and in what ways does it differ from "community"?

2. Whatever the differences, "unions of convenience" have the potential for community. What does that mean? Westley claims it is dangerous for people to gather for any reason because that potential is always there. What is so dangerous about community?

3. Give some examples from your own life, when what started out as a "union of convenience" turned into a "community" before it was over.

IV. Searching for Community

1. "There is a hunger abroad in the land, a hunger for the *human connection, intimacy,* and *a feeling of human solidarity.*"
Do you experience this hunger at all? How?

2. Is there really a "spiritual" famine in the land? What are its signs? How do you account for the fact that it doesn't seem to affect everybody? (Or does it?)

IV. Myths About Community

1. Myth 1: that community is a "thing," indeed a consumer good that other people can give me, which can be purchased like any other commodity.

Give some examples of the sorts of things people do trying to "buy" the human connection, intimacy, community.

What is your gut reaction to things like this? They can't hurt can they? And they just might help.

2. Myth 2: that community is a kind of utopia in which all relationships are supportive and without pain.

"There is no community without tears." Share some of the pain that you've experienced in community. What was its ultimate cause? How did you get through it? Was it worth it? In your judgment, why is community worth the struggle?

3. Myth 3: that community is the gathering of people who are compatible because they are alike in background and upbringing.

It would seem natural that people who are a lot alike and who are attracted to one another would cluster in groups. That is the natural outcome of friendship. Why doesn't that same principle work with regard to "community"?

V. Building Community

1. Community comes, Palmer says, as a by-product of commitment and struggle. It happens when we step forward:

a) to right some wrong,

b) to heal some hurt,

c) to resist the diminishments of life.

Share your experiences of having community happen around each of those items.

2. The question "Where can I find community?" is precisely

the wrong question. The right question is: "What are the prevailing diminishments in life that are currently crushing me and my sisters and brothers?" Why is the first question wrong-headed and the second one right-headed? What are the prevailing diminishments you're facing in your life right now? How about your sisters and brothers?

3. Comment on the thought that you don't "build" community so much as receive it as a "gift" when you are busy about something else.

VI. Community as Novitiate for Salvation/Reconciliation

1. "Community is as demanding as boot camp." Why? What are the most demanding aspects of community for you?

2. Why does Westley think that community is more difficult for people raised in the United States than elsewhere? Is this really the case? Why?

3. The fact is we are very ambivalent about community. We both hunger for it and fear it. Share some of your fears of it.

What are we so afraid of? Why?

4. Another paradox is the fact that the power of community really arises out of weakness and brokenness. What does this claim mean to you? Can you give any examples of how this works?

5. So long as we allow others no way into our brokenness, there can be no saving place for the individual, there can be no reconciliation for the world, there can be no life together.

Any reactions to this claim? Is it true? Westley thinks we can learn from Alcoholics Anonymous. What have you learned from them?

6. Comment on Westley's description of what it means to lose the faith:

Have we forgotten the malaise and deep hunger that spreads like famine across the earth? Have we forgotten despite all the obstacles, we humans have been made to live life together? That's who we are in our deepest parts. Have we forgotten that we are not alone, and that God is incarnated himself in human life precisely to keep it from fragmentation and disintegration, and that community among human beings is the result of this presence? And finally, have we forgotten the many women and men in our lives whose presence to and among us has witnessed to not only the possibility of community, but to its absolute inevitability? To have forgotten *all* of this is surely what it means to have lost the faith.

7. Are you losing the faith? If not, what keeps you hopeful and believing in the Kingdom enterprise?

CHAPTER SIX: THE "AMERICAN" ETHOS

I. Americanization

1. America is called the great melting pot, supposedly because it melts down all the ethnic differences of people and turns them into "Americans," whatever that means. What does that mean to you? Do you consider yourself to be typically American? Say why or why not.

2. Do you have any experience with recent immigrants? From what they tell you, what are the most difficult "adjustments" they have to make: a) in their heads or inner space? b) in their relations with others?

II. Elements of the "American" Character: A Look in the Mirror

Individualism

1. After observing Americans from 1835-1840, Alexis de Tocqueville wrote: "Individualism is a calm and considered feeling which disposes each citizen to isolate himself from the mass of his fellows and withdraw into the circle of family and friends; with this little society formed to his taste, he gladly leaves the greater society to look after itself." Any thoughts or reactions to this?

2. Bellah suggests that American individualism may have become cancerous, thus threatening the very life of liberty we all prize so much. Do you see any indications of this?

Share from your own experience what things indicate that our individualism is out of control.

3. The Latin writer Livy wrote about ancient Rome: "We have reached the point that we cannot bear either our vices or their cure." Are we Americans there yet?

4. What do you make of Bellah's distinction between *utilitarian individualism* and *expressive individualism*? How do they differ from one another? Which presents you with the greater challenge in your own life right now? How? Why?

5. It is suggested that these two types of individualism are really incompatible and that trying to achieve success in both ways leads to a lot of tension. Why is that? What is it about *utilitarian individualism* which opposes it to *expressive individualism*? How are you doing in putting it all together in your life?

Self-Reliance

1. We Americans tend to be self-reliant, and we teach our children to be that way too. What's wrong with this? "It's a hard cruel world out there and if you don't look after yourself who will? That's the trouble in America today, people expect hand-outs and 'free lunches'—we've lost the good old Yankee virtue of self-reliance." Comment on this statement.

2. Today self reliance seems to mean "the need to be self-sufficient, to be totally independent of and totally unencumbered by others." We speak less about a shared liberty these days, and more about personal individual freedom. Do you relate to this at all? Explain.

3. Westley says: "America's young people are being raised on the ideal of unencumbered self-reliance. They rush to "leave home," to "leave the church," to jettison the values of not only their parents and church but of their nation as well. They view any contribution from outside their autonomous selves as unwelcome and unjustified interference." Does this overstate the case? What has been your experience with the young?

Reaping the Fruits of Our National Character
Work: "American Style"

1. Until very recently, the old "work ethic" was the prevailing American value system. Some say that is no longer the case. What is the old American "work ethic"? And what signs do you see that it is on the wane?

2. Much of the work we are asked to do is so trivial or meaningless that it is difficult to put our hearts into it. One dreams of the weekend, the next coffee break, the next party, the next cruise, the next ski trip, the next vacation. Anything to get out of work. Any comments on this?

3. Bellah views "work" from three different perspectives. Explain what he means by each, and comment on his view from your own experience. Sharing perhaps what is was like when you had a "job," when you had a "career." Have you ever experienced your work as a "calling"?

a) Work as job...(producing a utilitarian self-image)

b) Work as career...(producing also an expressive self-image)

c) Work as calling...(gets us somehow beyond individualism

4. The competition and pressures of the business world are fierce and unrelenting, always the bottom line. Does working in this sort of atmosphere hinder you at all in relating to friends and family after work hours? What would your spouse or children have to say about this?

III. Therapy: The American Way of Presence

1. Have you ever been in therapy or counseling? Was it a good experience? If so, share what you can about how it made you feel and why in retrospect you still judge it to have been a good experience.

2. If you've never had the experience, say how you feel about people who have. Do you see them as weak? As sick? As unsuccessful? If not, since that's the stereotype, when and why did you come to see things differently?

3. Comment on the following: "The 'cure' people seek from therapists is some way to empower the individual self to be able to cope with the often conflicting demands of work and intimacy. Somehow, they feel impotent in the face of the overwhelming social pressures inherent in our way of life."

4. From all accounts, people often feel that time with their therapist is sacred time, and that their sessions are really a sort of "religious" experience. Any comments?

5. Therapy is often seen as a "saving place." How can that be if in the end it reinforces expressive individualism? Can salvation be an individual event?

6. Westley says that one reason people prefer therapy to religion is that the therapist leaves them in control, works for their freedom and well-being, while religion attempts to encumber them. What do you make of this? What does it mean to be "unencumbered"? To be "encumbered"?

IV. Lifestyle vs. Community

1. What do you make of Bellah's distinction between *lifestyle enclaves* and *community*? What do you understand him to be saying about what makes them different?

2. What makes lifestyle enclaves so attractive to us Americans is that it leaves us in control. We group with people who have no claim on us, we remain unencumbered. Identify some of the lifestyle enclaves to which you belong. Assess their contribution to your life.

3. Identify a "community" you belong to, and contrast the way you are present there to the way you are present in your lifestyle enclaves. Have you ever been in a lifestyle enclave that turned into a community? If so, share how this worked.

4. Is your parish a "community" or a "lifestyle enclave"? How can you tell? What are the criteria for deciding that?

V. Love: "American Style"

1. What do you think accounts for the growing divorce rate in America? What in your mind is the major contributing factor?

2. What is your reaction to Bellah's claim that: "American individualism has difficulty justifying why men and women should be giving themselves to one another at all."

3. How do you feel about contemporary marriages with two incomes and no kids? Having a family has become *optional*. Isn't that the way it should be?

VI. Contemporary America: A Critique

1. Tocqueville foresaw the disintegration of our national life if individualism went unchecked. He identified three other elements in American life that would keep individualism in check and from becoming destructive. They are: *religion, marriage and family,* and *public service.*

a) What do you perceive to be the state of religion in America today? What do you make of the claim that instead of mitigating individualism, religion where it exists at all has itself been subverted by it?

b) What do you perceive to be the state of married life and family in America today? Individualism now pervades family life and marriage, so these things can no longer be viewed as checks on it. Any thoughts?

c) What do you perceive is the state of public service in America today? Who even thinks of entering it these days? And what do their friends and family tell those who think of doing it?

2. Given the present state of affairs in America, perhaps Pope John Paul II has a point in criticizing the American church. He sees us as shot through with self-reliance and individualism, wanting to reduce the church to a personal "enhancement" of some sort. We want our way. He has vowed to not let that happen. Isn't that what a pope ought to do? What is your position on this?

VII. The American Experience as Revelatory

1. Does "being an American" ever conflict with your "being a Christian/Catholic"? If so explain where the conflict arises and how you cope with it. If not, say why.

2. If experience is "revelatory," what do all these negatives in American experience reveal to you? What insights do those experiences give you?

CHAPTER SEVEN: A PERSONAL INTERLUDE

I. Reflecting on the Parable

1. Try to quiet your head for the moment. How many different "feelings" can you identify yourself as having experienced during the reading of the parable? (Remember: "emotions" *not* "thoughts.")

As you came to the end of the parable, what was the lasting and predominant "feeling" that stayed with you?

2. Every good parable contains many interesting "themes" and "insights," but ultimately only one "message." What were the "themes" and "insights" you found clustered around the character of:

a) the priest?

b) the young girl?

c) the Buddhist monk?

3. As with all good parables, this one is filled with meaning. What do you think it means? That is, what is its central message? In any event, what message did you take away from it? Explain.

4. Sullivan named his little piece *A Parable,* and Westley took the liberty of changing it to *A "Catholic" Parable: A Love Story.* The parable is obviously a love story, but did it reveal anything to you about "being a Catholic"? What?

CHAPTER EIGHT: THE "CATHOLIC" ETHOS

I. General Issues

1. Westley seems to think that Rome is leaning on the American church and he gives several instances of what he means. Perhaps you could comment on each of them:

a) He claims that American bishops are under duress, and speaks of a couple of them as operating under what amounts to "house arrest."

i) Do you have any indications that **your** bishop is operating under any sort of unusual pressure coming from Rome these days? Explain.

ii) When Westley speaks of "house arrest" he obviously has Archbishop Hunthausen of Seattle in mind. What are your reactions to the Hunthausen case? Did it cause any reactions in your diocese?

b) As for American theologians being under attack, obviously Westley has the Fr. Charles Curran case in mind. Were there any reactions to that case in your diocese? What do you know about it? Where are you with regard to it?

c) There seems to be a deep-seated hurt and anger among women in the church over Pope John Paul II's absolute intransigence on the woman's issue. Where are you on the issue of the ordination of women? What is the mood or attitude of the women in your parish with regard to the institutional church these days? Is that a change from, say, five years ago? Explain.

2. Are the Catholics you know energetic and enthusiastic about their faith or are they showing signs of discouragement? Are you discouraged these days? If so, say why.

3. What were your reactions to Pope John Paul II's visit to the United States in the fall of 1987? Westley claims it had a "chilling effect." Did it for you? Explain.

4. What are your reactions to the banning of the "C-word" from school premises by the principal in Alaska? What else could he do? Westley says this is a portent of things to come. What do you see coming?

5. Given the present tone of American culture, Westley thinks that perhaps the pope has some justification for thinking that the American Catholic church is out of control, in open disobedience, and perhaps even in schism. What do you think? Or do we just look that way to him because the church has suddenly become very, very legalistic? Where are you on this issue?

6. On the whole, do you find the Catholics of your diocese to be good, God-fearing people, truly committed to the Christian enterprise? Or do you find them succumbing to the blandishments of our self-seeking culture and hence deserving of the criticisms of Rome?

7. When you look around your parish or diocese, do you see lots of faces missing? What accounts for that, do you think?

What about looking around your family? Have family members separated themselves from church in growing numbers? Why? What are your reactions to this?

II. A Matter of Conscience

1. The Catholic tradition is replete with beautiful and startling statements about human freedom. Share your reactions to:

a) The quote from the Book of Sirach (15:14)

b) The quote from the Prophet Jeremiah (31:31-33)

c) The quotes from Thomas Aquinas.

d) The quote from Pope Pius XII.

e) The quotes from the Second Vatican Council.

2. That part of our tradition isn't mentioned much, and certainly isn't stressed. Could that be because we Americans are already too intoxicated with freedom? Has anyone shared that part of our tradition with you? Who? Explain.

3. Westley claims that the tradition is clear, but that all too often it is just words, beautiful words, but just words nonetheless. We are afraid to preach "freedom." Why, do you think?

4. Jesus was human, so he knew fear. But Westley claims he never feared freedom. Cite some gospel stories that either corroborate or undermine this statement.

5. What do you understand by the phrase "freedom of conscience"?

What does it mean to you? Are there any limits to freedom or is it absolute? How do you relate "freedom of conscience" to church laws?

6. When church law and your conscience don't agree, how do you go about resolving the issue? Be specific. What process do you go through in attempting to discover what is the right thing to do?

7. To obey a law you don't believe in is inauthentic. To leave the church because you cannot honestly obey when you know you are called to be Catholic is also inauthentic. What a mess ! Any thoughts of a solution?

8. To follow one's conscience is not at all the same thing as *doing one's own thing* , following individual whim or fancy. What evidence do you have from your own lived experience to substantiate this claim? (Recall: We are not alone; God *is* present to us.)

III. Conscience as "Catholic"

1. From what you know of them, what makes Daniel Berrigan, Theresa Kane, and Mary Agnes Mansour "believers of conscience"? Where are they with respect to the law? Are they "disobedient" or "schismatic" in your eyes?

What about the ancient prophets of Israel? In this context what do you have to say about them?

2. What does it mean to say that conscience, in its very nature, is "catholic"?

3. Just as the God of Exodus is different from the God of Genesis, so Westley distinguishes two kinds of conscience, the one he calls a "Genesis-conscience," the other an "Exodus-conscience." What is he getting at? What is the difference between them?

4. Westley implies that the reason for the conflict between the church in Rome and the American church is that the one operates out of a "Genesis-conscience" and the other out of an "Exodus-conscience." What do you think of approaching the present conflict in the church this way?

IV. Why Be Catholic?

1. Why be Catholic? Everyone has his or her own answer to this difficult question. What's yours?

2. Comment and evaluate the significance of each of the following answers to our question. It is important to be a Catholic:

a)...because the Catholic church is the one true church.

b) ...because it has all seven of the sacraments, especially the Mass and Eucharist.

c) ...because the pope is infallible in matters of faith and morals and the very vicar of Christ on earth.

d) and finally...because it is the church founded by Christ who is the savior of the world and membership in it is the best guarantee of one's eternal salvation.

3. Catholic ethos is one of "universality," everyone is in despite diversity. And Westley says that the genius of the Catholic ethos is that in the name of religious liberty people can remain within the community *while disagreeing*. What are your reactions to that view of the Catholic ethos?

4. Many, many Americans have left the church. Why does he think this is exactly the wrong time to think of leaving the church?

5. It is claimed that the old "catholic" (read: parochial) reality is dying and a whole new "catholic" reality is aborning. What does this mean to you? What do you see aborning? How will the new "catholic" reality differ from the traditional one? Does your experience cause you to agree or disagree? Is it true that the present repressive measures from Rome are signs of desperation? Can the new thing be stopped, do you think?

6. Westley gives several reasons why one should be Catholic. What is your evaluation of them:

a)...because the Catholic ethos is the ethos of our time and truly speaks future.

b)...because the Catholic church is the only religious institution that on its own principles can say *it really doesn't matter!*

c) ...because if one lives long enough and gives heed to what life teaches, one comes to see that the Catholic ethos is corroborated by experience and that *it really doesn't matter!*

d) ...because those who are Catholic, precisely because *it really doesn't matter,* are at liberty to be what they are, and to become even more authentic "Catholics."

7. Recall that Westley renamed Francis Sullivan's *"A Parable,"* calling it *"A Catholic" Parable."* Does having read this section cast any more light on why he might have done that? What about the parable is so particularly "Catholic" in your eyes?

V. What Does Matter?

1. To say "it really doesn't matter" is not to say that nothing matters. What is it that matters? What is it that doesn't matter according to Westley?

2. Comment on the following: "What doesn't matter refers to all those things that human ingenuity has devised to divide people from one another."

3. What are some of the things that "religion" has invented to divide people from one another? What are some of the things that governments and nations (nationalism) have invented to needlessly divide the human race?

4. Westley claims that the American dream at its best, and the Catholic dream at its best, are really the same dream. What do you make of this? This would mean that the American dream was basically "catholic." Does this make any sense to you?

5. Two events in recent history stand out as witnessing to the new reality that is aborning and of being truly "catholic," i.e. the Camp David Accord, and Pope John Paul II's convening of religious leaders at Assisi to pray for world peace. Any thoughts?

6. Westley wrote a prayer in which he tried to sum up what he was feeling as he ended the book. Now that you have read the book yourself, why don't you write a concluding prayer.

NOTES

1. Throughout this book, I have referred to the "American" church, meaning, of course, the church in the United States. This conventional use of the word "American" is not meant to be offensive to citizens of any of the other Americas north or south, and should be understood in the context in which it is being used, that is, to refer to that cultural phenomenon of Western industrial and post-industrial capitalism of which the United States has been, until recently, the pre-eminent model. So much so that it is no exaggeration to say the "American" dream has become the prevailing dream of secular cultures throughout the world.

2. Soren Kierkegaard, *Philosophical Fragments*, ed. Hong and Hong (Princeton, N.J.: Princeton University Press, 1985).

3. Gabriel Marcel, *The Mystery of Being* (South Bend: Gateway Editions, 1978), Vol. I, p. 205.

4. Daniel Berrigan, S.J., "On Nuclear Terror," a talk given at Loyola University in New Orleans, June 27, 1983.

5. Augustus Napier and Carl Whitaker, *The Family Crucible* (New York: Bantam Books, 1980), p. 123.

6. Robert Tyler, "The Two-Marriage, Revolving-Mate, Generating Bridging Plan To Save Marriage," in *The Humanist* (November/December, 1970), pp. 30-31.

7. Robert Bellah, *Habits of the Heart* (New York: Harper & Row, 1985), p. 111.

8. Virginia Satir, *Conjoint Family Therapy: A Guide to Theory and Techniques* (Palo Alto: Science & Behavior Books, 1967), pp. 1-7.

9. I didn't know this as I read the book, so it came as something of a revelation to me at the time. And though my revealing the "ending" may deprive you of the same sort of revelatory experience I had in reading it, I think it should be required reading for all couples, be they parents or not.

10. I find it instructive to note that if we list the popes since the declar-

ation of papal infallibility (Pius IX, Leo XIII, Pius X, Benedict XV, Pius XI, Pius XII, John XXIII, Paul VI, John Paul I, and John Paul II) the most authoritative and hence most effective of those great pontiffs was undoubtedly John XXIII. Indeed, so long as John XXIII remains in memory, Catholics will not wholeheartedly accept any other kind of pope-ing. Roncalli so endeared himself to people that he was not only pope of Catholics, but of the whole world. In him the whole world saw incarnated what popes should be, and having seen the truth in the flesh, we can no longer be satisfied with anything less. But alas, the way things are going who can say for how long good Pope John will remain in memory?

11. Alphonse Spilly, "Sin and Alienation in the Old Testament: The Personalist Approach," *Chicago Studies*, 21, (Fall 1982), pp. 211-225.

12. Parker Palmer, *The Promise of Paradox* (Notre Dame: Ave Maria Press, 1980), p. 56.

13. Aristotle, *Politics*, I, 1.

14. Parker Palmer, *op. cit*, p. 80.

15. Robert Bellah, *op. cit.* Bellah's book became a national best seller because it is written in everyday language and not the usual jargon of social theorists. But it has been widely criticized by American sociologists because it is not value-free, and dares to speak affirmingly of the importance of moral and religious values for our national life. It is a landmark book that should be read in every high school and college in the nation. It holds up a mirror to our current values, compares them with the values that prevailed at the birth of our country, and suggests ways in which we can both keep the best of our traditional values and continue to move into the twenty-first century. Personally, I continue to be nourished from my reading of it years later, seeing ever more clearly in myself and in those around me the elements that make us typically "American" in character.

16. Alexis de Tocqueville, *Democracy in America* (New York: Doubleday, 1969).

17. Louis Evely, *If the Church Is to Survive* (New York: Doubleday, 1972), pp. 80, 83.

18. Thomas Aquinas, "Prologue to Prima Secundae" of the *Summa Theologiae*.

19. Thomas Aquinas, *Summa Theologiae* I-II, 91, 2, c.

20. Pius XII, Radio Broadcast of March 23, 1952.

21. Vatican II, *The Church in the Modern World,* #41.

22. Vatican II, *On Religious Freedom,* #13.

INDEX